Charles Chauncy

Breaking of Bread

in remembrance of the dying Love of Christ

Charles Chauncy

Breaking of Bread
in remembrance of the dying Love of Christ

ISBN/EAN: 9783337159108

Printed in Europe, USA, Canada, Australia, Japan

Cover: Foto ©Lupo / pixelio.de

More available books at **www.hansebooks.com**

"Breaking of Bread," in remembrance of the dying Love of Chriſt, a Goſpel inſtitution.

FIVE SERMONS.

In which the inſtitution is explained; a general obſervance of it recommended and enforced; objections anſwered; and ſuch Difficulties, Doubts, and Fears, relative to it, particularly mentioned, and removed, which have too commonly diſcouraged ſome from an attendance at it, and proved to others a ſource of diſcomfort, in the regard they have endeavoured to pay to it.

BY

Charles Chauncy, D. D.

Pastor of the first Church of Christ in Boston.

BOSTON:

Printed by D. Kneeland, in Queen-Street, for Thomas Leverett, in Corn-hill.

M,DCC,LXXII.

"Breaking of Bread," in remembrance of CHRIST, a Gospel-duty.

Acts. II. 42.

"*And they continued stedfastly—in breaking of
"Bread.*"

THE preceeding verses contain an account of the sermon, which the apostle Peter preached to a great auditory of Jews, by descent, or proselitism, collected at Jerusalem on the day of Pentecost. By means of this sermon, multitudes had awakened in them such a sense of sin

and

and guilt, as, in good earnest, to make that inquiry "men and brethren what shall we do"? Upon which, the apostle Peter directed them to " repent, and be baptised every one of them in the name of Jesus Christ for the remission of sins." We are then told, that no less than " three thousand persons gladly received the word, were baptised, and added to the number of disciples". It follows, in the words of my text, that they " continued stedfastly—in breaking of bread."

The "bread" which they are said to "break" undoubtedly means the *sacramental bread*, that bread which is an instituted sign or symbol, of the " body of Christ which was broken for us." Some indeed seem to think it was only common bread; but to me it appears strange, they should give it this sense. It is true, " the bread" these christians are spoken of, ver. 46, as " daily breaking from house to house," may mean common bread; for it is joined with their " eating meat" for their bodily refreshment. And, if it is natural, from the things con-joined in this verse, to understand by the " bread they brake," common bread; it is equally natural, in the verse we are upon, to understand the same phrase in a different sense; not as meaning common, but sacramental bread.

For

For the other actions here mentioned are sacred ones. And as this of "breaking bread" is joined with a "continuance in the apostle's doctrine and prayers," which are instances of communion in "things pertaining to the kingdom of God, and of Jesus Christ," it would be unreasonable to interpret it as signifying, in this place, nothing more than that "breaking of bread" which is common and ordinary: Especially if it be remembered, that "breaking of bread," meaning hereby celebrating the Lord's-Supper, was a religious exercise, in which christians, in apostolic times, joined together every Lord's day, with like steadiness as in their attendance on the word preached, or prayer.

It is accordingly not only said, in my text, that they "break bread"; but that they "stedfastly continued" to do so. The meaning is, it was a constant part of their public worship, one of their stated religious exercises, a duty which they went on in the practice of; persevering therein with the same steadiness with which they observed the other instituted services of piety. *

FROM

---

* As "breaking of bread" in apostolic times, was one of the known christian exercises on Lord's-Days, it may be

From the words, as they have been explained, I am obviously led to urge upon christian professors the duty of "breaking bread" at the Lord's table; and this I shall the more readily engage in, as it is a duty, to whatever cause it may be asked, is not this a duty now as truly as it was then? And are not christian Churches to blame, that they do not "break bread" every Lord's-day, in remembrance of their Lord? In answer hereto, it is readily allowed, that on Lord's-days, it was the practice of christians, in the age of the apostles, to "break bread", as well as to attend on other parts of gospel worship. But I dare not venture to say, it will follow from hence, that christian churches are all bound to do as they did. A distinction ought always to be made betwixt that which is *essential*, and that which is *circumstantial*, in any article of duty. To "break bread" in remembrance of Christ, is *essentially* a christian duty; the *special frequency* of doing this is a *circumstance* only, which it may be proper should be varied, according to the state of christian churches. Our Lord has said, "This do in remembrance of me"; but neither he, nor any of his apostles, have said, this do *every Lord's-day*. The practice of christian churches in the days of the apostles, especially with them joining in it, is, it is acknowledged, a weighty consideration, and every way sufficient to put it beyond all doubt, that the supper of the Lord ought to be attended with *frequency*; and those churches are herefrom justly, and strongly rebuked, who " break Bread" not oftener than *once*, or *twice*, or *thrice*, in a whole year. But to argue from this practice of the primitive christians, that it is an indispensible duty to have the sacramental supper every Lord's-day, may be carrying the argument beyond which it will fairly, or justly, bear. Perhaps, no practice of any church, or of

any

may be owing, that is greatly neglected in these days. Multitudes of those who call themselves chriſtians, inſtead of celebrating the ſacramental ſupper, go from it as though they had no concern in it, or as if it were a trifling inſtitution, not worth their regard. The neglect of "eating bread, and drinking wine," in remembrance of him who died for our ſins, is indeed grown a general fault, and juſtly chargeable upon baptiſed

any apoſtle, or of all the apoſtles united, ſeparate from a *divine command*, direct or implicit, is abſolutely binding upon any ſociety of chriſtians whatever. It may be of great ſervice in guiding their conduct, but not certainly obligatory in point of conſcience; to be ſure, not ſo in all caſes, and at all times. There may be ſuch a variety, yea, contrariety, in the ſtate and circumſtances of churches, as not to make that expedient, which is not commanded, though it ſhould have been a primitive practice, and a commendable one too. And it is, beyond all diſpute, true, that the *command*, reſpecting the ſacramental ſupper, relates to doing the duty itſelf, preſcribing nothing in particular as to the *frequency* of its being performed; whether every day, or week, or month, or year. In general, it may be juſtly collected from the practice of the firſt chriſtians, eſpecially when compared with thoſe words of the apoſtle Paul, "as oft as ye do this," that the ſupper of the Lord ought to be celebrated with *ſuch frequency*, as that it may, with propriety, be ſaid, it is done *often*. I judge no chriſtian church for "breaking bread" every Lord's-Day: Neither ought they to judge other churches, who think, if they *often* do this, it is all they are obliged to, in virtue of any PRECEPT in the religion of Jeſus,

tified perſons arrived at maturity of age and underſtanding. It is a ſhame it ſhould be thus, a reproach upon chriſtians, a diſhonour to the religion they profeſs, and an open and ſcandalous affront to him whom they own to be their Maſter and Lord. How different is the practice of diſciples now from what it was in the days of the apoſtles! An attendance at the ſacramental table was then UNIVERSAL among thoſe who profeſſed faith in Jeſus Chriſt. Among the three thouſand perſons, ſpoken of, in the context, as admitted to baptiſm, there was not one that did not communicate alſo at the Lord's-Supper; and it was their conſtant practice to do ſo. This noble example of the primitive chriſtians, recorded to their honor by an inſpired pen, may, with all reaſon, be eſteemed a ſolemn rebuke of that negligence, in regard of the Lord's-Supper, which is now become almoſt univerſal. And I may properly, and not unſeaſonably, take occaſion from it to repreſent to all that " name the name of Chriſt" the ſinfulneſs of ſuch neglect, by opening to their view, in the plaineſt and ſtrongeſt manner I am able, the ſolemn bonds they are under to attend as gueſts at the ſacramental table.

THEY are obliged to this by the poſitive command of Jeſus Chriſt, the founder of our religion

religion, and the author of falvation. He has folemnly enjoined it on all, who own themfelves his difciples, to "break bread" in honor to him. THIS DO IN REMEMBRANCE OF ME, are the words of his command: Nor could he have expreffed his pleafure upon this head in terms more plain and explicit. They lie level to the loweft capacity, and may readily be underftood by all that do not fhut their eyes againft the light.

SHOULD it be faid here, the mind of Chrift, tis true, was plainly enough fignified to his apoftles, making it their duty to " break bread and eat it, to pour out wine and drink it in remembrance of him"; but it is not fo evident, that this command to them was, in the defign of Chrift, an obligation upon difciples in general.

IT is readily acknowledged, the words of inftitution were originally fpoken to the twelve apoftles only; for which reafon, it cannot be certainly argued, from the words themfelves fimply confidered, that chriftians in general are obliged to celebrate this memorial of Chrift's death. The apoftles might be applied to in their proper charaƈter as fuch, or as difciples only; and whether it was in the former, or latter of thefe fenfes, cannot be determined

by

by the meer force of our Lord's words, as they were delivered by him. But this notwithstanding, it is not, in any degree, uncertain, whether our Savior intended, by the words he spake to his apostles, to oblige christians in common, as well as his apostles in particular, to attend at the sacramental supper. For it is to be remembered, the apostles were infallible interpreters of our Lord's words; insomuch that we may, with intire confidence, depend on the truth they construe them in. And nothing in all the bible is more clearly and indubitably evident than this, that they accounted the Lord's-Supper an established rite of gospel-worship, an institution of Christ, that all his professed disciples were as truly obliged to observe as they themselves. Why else was it the practice of christians in their day, and by their order, to join in partaking of the symbols of Christ's death? Three thousand persons, upon being baptised by the apostles, were, in one day, admitted to sit down with them at the Lord's-Supper; and they "continued" to do so, wherever this ordinance was administred; as we read in my text and context. And it is beyond all dispute evident, not only that christians in common met together every Lord's-Day to join in prayer, and an attendance

on

on the word preached; but in "breaking of bread" also, a phrase that means the same thing precisely with their celebration of the sacramental supper. And they did this under the eye of the apostles, with them at their head, and as acting under their guidance and direction. Surely, they would not have thus put christians upon partaking of the Lord's-Supper, and have joined with them in it, had they not known the mind of their master upon this head. It was unquestionably his intention, in the appointment of the supper, to oblige all the professors of his religion to an observance of it: Otherwise, this conduct of the apostles, who were constituted by him infallible guides and teachers, will be absolutely unaccountable. Besides, it may be worthy of remark, when the apostle Paul found the christians at Corinth in the use of this act of religious worship, he does not forbid their going on in it, as being a duty proper to apostles only. It is true, he blames them for the irregularities they had mixed with their use of this ordinance; but not for their use of the ordinance itself. Far from this, he solemnly assures them, as from Jesus Christ himself, that the sacramental supper was a sacred rite of gospel worship, instituted by our Saviour himself for the use of all christians. And, as the best remedy to cure their disorders, he relates to them the institution itself, and directs them to manage their attendance on it in strict agreement therewith.

So that, upon the whole, it will not admit of debate, whether " eating bread and drinking wine, in remembrance of Christ," is an established rite of his religion. It is as obviously and certainly an institution of the gospel as " baptism in the name of the Father, and of " the Son, and of the holy Ghost", or indeed any law recorded in the new-testament.

THERE is therefore, so far as we regard the authority of Jesus Christ, the same reason why we should " break bread," in remembrance of him, as that we should obey him in any other instance of duty whatever. Why do we think ourselves obliged to join as christians, in observing the Lord's-Day, or in attending on the word preached and prayer? Is it that we might be obedient to Jesus Christ, who is king in Sion? We are equally under obligation to celebrate the memorial of his death. This ordinance has the same stamp of his authority on it; nor are we any more at liberty to disregard it in this instance, than in the other. Nay, if we knowingly, and habitually offend in this point, we may reasonably
call

call in question the integrity of our hearts respecting the other. He that has said, "repent and be baptised," neglect not the assembling yourselves together "for the services of piety, such as prayer, reading and hearing God's word, has said also, and in words equally authoritative, " this do in remembrance of me." And if we practically slight the authority of Christ in this latter instance, why should we think our regards to it are pure and single as to the former? The plain truth is, the Commands of Jesus Christ are all given out with the same authority. And if this authority obliges us to obedience in any, it does in every instance. We have no right to make exceptions, doing one thing, and leaving another undone. The only question here is, has Jesus Christ, who is Head and Lord of his church, instituted the sacramental supper? Has he commanded his disciples to "eat bread and drink wine in remembrance of him"? If his will, in this matter, has been plainly made known, an end is at once put to all dispute. It is our indispensible duty to honour his authority, by readily complying with his Command.

AND, I may pertinently add here, there are some circumstances attending this command in special,

special, which are powerfully suited to awaken our consideration, and excite in us a care of punctual obedience to it.

It is a command that has been carefully preserved, and faithfully handed down to us, by no less than three of the Evangelists. Surely, the Spirit of God, under whose extraordinary influence these holy men were moved to write the gospels, esteemed the sacramental supper an appointment of no small importance, and had it in view to bind the celebration of it upon the disciples of Christ in the strongest manner. Had the words, in which our Lord instituted the memorial of his death, been transmitted to us by one of the sacred penmen only, they would have been obligatory upon all who own Christ for their master; But, as they have been repeatedly conveyed, the obligation is more unquestionable, we are more firmly bound to pay a religious regard to this instance of duty; and if we neglect to do so, the guilt hereby incurred will be greatly heightened. A serious thought this! and it were to be wished it might be seriously attended to by all who profess themselves christians.

Another circumstance attending the command we are upon, worthy of particular notice, is, the *extraordinary manner* in which it
was

was conveyed to the apostle Paul. It should be remembered here, he was not an apostle, nor so much as a believer, when our Lord injoined "the eating of bread, and drinking of wine" in commemoration of him. It was after this time, and years too, that he became a convert to the religion of Jesus, and a fellow-laborer with the other apostles in the gospel-kingdom. And now it was that he received the knowledge of the sacramental institution. But how did he receive it? "not of men, neither was he taught it but by the revelation of Jesus Christ." So he expresly assures us himself. Says he, 1 Cor. 11. 23, "I received of "the Lord that which also I delivered unto "you, that the Lord Jesus, the same night in "which he was betrayed, took bread, and "brake it, and said, take, eat, this is my body "which is broken for you; this do in remem- "brance of me."—The prefixed words, "I "received of the Lord," were evidently intended to point out the way in which he came by the knowledge of the supper, as a divine appointment; that it was, not by instruction from the other apostles, nor by any communication that was meerly human; but from Jesus Christ himself. And may it not from hence be fairly concluded, that the sacramental institution was, in the esteem of our Lord, a matter of solemn weight, and that he would by no means have it disregarded? Why else should he make a revelation of it to the apostle Paul immediately from heaven? His taking this extraordinary method certainly argues the singular importance of the duty, and renders it an inexcuseable fault in christians to live in the neglect of it.

There is yet another momentous circumstance, accompanying the command to "break bread" in remembrance of Christ. And this is, the time when it was first given out. The apostle Paul takes notice of this circumstance, and puts a special emphasis on it. His words are, "THE SAME NIGHT IN WHICH HE WAS BETRAYED the Lord Jesus took bread, and said, take eat, this is my body which is broken for you: This do in remembrance of me." Surely, no matter of trifling consideration would have engaged the attention of our Saviour at such a time as this! He would not, at so serious and solemn a juncture, have injoined this duty, and by his own example have shewed his disciples how to perform it, if he had not tho't it worthy of particular regard, and supposed that his followers would think so too. He too well understood human nature, not to mean some special

cial recommendation of the sacramental supper by instituting it at so critical a time. In a dying hour, the most earnest desires of the soul are wont to be expressed; and to such desires the greatest regard is commonly paid. If a command, or request, comes from a dying man, especially if he is a friend, a benefactor, whom we love, honour and admire, it is apt deeply to impress our minds, nor can we easily hear it with indifference and neglect. Such now, though in a much higher sense, is the command to "break bread" at the sacramental table. It is the fare-well-request, the last injunction, the dying charge, not only of our best friend, and greatest benefactor; but of him whom we call our Master and Lord. Shall we any of us, after this, habitually neglect the institution of the supper? Shall we express, in our practice, a disregard to a duty, constituted such by the blessed Jesus, just as he was going to lay down his life for us? How shall we free ourselves from the charge of base ingratitude to the greatest lover of our souls, if we reckon it a frivolous rite, or are wanting in our care to pay all due honour to it? Especially, as it was injoined under circumstances, so peculiarly fitted 'to strike our minds, work upon our passions, and engage our religious observance

vance of it. May it not be reasonably questioned, whether we mind our Lord's other commands, if we can easily, carelesly, and habitually forget, in our practice, this, which was his last and dying one, and delivered with so much particularity and solemnity?

I HAVE hitherto argued from the authority only by which the Lord's-Supper was instituted. If we go on, and consider the design of this ordinance, and the good effects it is fitted to produce, we shall find ourselves under strong additional obligations readily to pay our dutiful regard to it.

WE may be apt to speak of it as nothing more than an injoined ritual that has no intrinsic value in it. And it is acknowledged, it is not, in itself simply considered, a natural, essential, inseperable part of religion, as the love of God and our neighbour; but a positive institution, dependant on the will of Jesus Christ. But it may notwithstanding be an important useful appointment. We have seen, from several circumstances already mentioned, that our Lord himself entertained this thought of it; and we may be further assured of this, from its being his appointment, though he had abolished all the rites and ceremonies of the Jewish law. Surely, he would not have
made

made the "breaking and eating of bread," in a certain way, a sacred rite of christianity, if he had not thought it highly expedient ; if the design in view had not been valuable, and the tendency of the thing good likewise in itself.

As to the design of the sacramental institution, it was to perpetuate, by visible symbols, the memory of a crucified Saviour. "This do in remembrance of me". The thing meant is, not meerly that christians, when partaking of the Lord's-Supper, should employ their thoughts on the sufferings of him who died for them. This, no doubt, was one thing intended, and expected ; and it would be highly misbecoming, if, while at this solemnity, they did not keep in mind, and seriously contemplate, the love of their Savior, who " died for sin, the just for the unjust, that he might bring us to God." But more than this was in the view of Christ, when he appointed the Gospel-Supper. His intention was, that this should be celebrated, in the assemblies of christians, as an open declarative representation of his death. " It is one thing, says an excellent writer, in-
" wardly to remember, and another to cele-
" brate, and solemnly to exhibit, a public me-
" memorial, by which we not only remember
" a fact, but avowedly and triumphantly pro-
" claim

"claim our remembrance, and our desire to have that remembrance observed, upheld and propagated," In this sense, the Lord's-Supper was appointed for a declaration, or "shewing forth of Christ's death." The separation of bread and wine at the sacrament, the breaking and eating the one, and the pouring out and drinking the other, do, according to the nature of signs, figuratively set forth, that Christ's body was broken and bruised, and his blood shed as an atonement for sin. This is what is meant by these signs, and they are made easie and intelligible to the most vulgar capacity by the words themselves, which not only relate the institution, but explain its sense; as in the passover, Exod. 12. 25—27, the memorial was exhibited, and the sense of it given.

WHEN therefore our Savior appointed the breaking and eating of bread, and pouring out and drinking of wine, "in remembrance of him," he not only intended this as an occasion for the meditation of christians on his crucifixtion and death, but for preserving, and transmitting, the memorial of so important an event from age to age, even to the end of the world. Thus the passover was a memorial throughout the whole time the Jewish law was in force. And thus the Supper of the Lord, celebrated

by

by christians in the manner he has prescribed, is an open public declaration of his dying love, perpetuating the memory of that amazing event, which is the true basis of all our hopes of forgiveness with God. By means of this monument, the memory of Christ's death for the salvation of a miserable world has been hitherto preserved. and will be handed down to the end of the world. So great and valuable a design was in the view of Christ, when he appointed the sacramental supper !

AND shall we any of us be backward in comporting with so glorious an intention ? How dwelleth the love of Christ in us, if we have no perception of a readiness to take occasion, from the instituted signs of his body broken, and his blood shed, to keep up in our minds the memory of his death ? If we can allowedly go out of the assemblies of christians, not joining with them in recognising, and perpetuating the memorial of the greatest event that ever took place in our world, and that is closely connected too with the salvation of it ? We are obliged to nothing, if we are not obliged, in the way of Christ's appointment, to celebrate the memory of his death.

BUT besides the bonds we are under to appear as guests at the Lord's-Supper from the
valuable

valuable end designed by its appointment, we are further obliged to this duty in consideration of its advantageous tendency, suitably regarded. It is an appointment of mercy, powerfully adapted to produce spiritually good effects; and cannot fail of doing so, unless it be our own fault. The bread which is broken at this ordinance is an instituted sign that has this meaning, the body of Christ was wounded when he stood in our place, and bore our iniquities. The wine that is poured out is an emblematical figure signifying, that his blood was shed for the remission of sins. And can we eat of this bread, and drink of this wine, in this view of them, and not receive benefit herefrom? The greatest occasion is hereby given for the excitement, and exercise, of all the passions and affections of the human mind; and if our thoughts are suitably engaged and employed, great good will be the effect; and this, whether we are the subjects of a common faith only, or of that faith which is saving.

If we have, at present, no other faith than that which is the result of serious inquiry, under the common influence of the divine Spirit, which was the only faith of multitudes who partook of the Lord's-Supper, in the days of the apostles, this ordinance is happily calcula-
lated

ted and suited to promote our good. More powerful considerations to this end cannot be proposed to us, than those that obviously present themselves at the sacramental table. Here the love of the Father is figuratively set forth to us in the strongest point of light. Wherein could he, in a more striking manner, have commended his love to us, than by sending his Son to die for us, while we were yet sinners? And who, that is in a serious frame of mind, can think of this amazing love of God, and not feel the emotions of affection towards him?—Here also the love of Christ is kindly held out to our view. Would he have laid down his life for us, if he had not loved us with a love stronger than death? And what can constrain us to live, not to ourselves, but to him, if this love of his in dying for us has no influence on us?—Here likewise the just desert of sin is, in the most lively manner, pointed out to us. Would the only Son of God have had laid on him such a load of sufferings, if sin had not been meritorious of the high displeasure of almighty God? And if he suffered so much, while he only stood in our place, how shall we escape, if we will not be persuaded to leave our sins? The reasoning of our Saviour upon this head is easie and just, and muſt ſtrike our minds with force, if we will attend to it, "if they do theſe things in a green tree, what ſhall be done in the dry"? Luk. 23. 31. In a word, we have here preached to us with great plainneſs, though in figurative ſigns, reconciliation with God through the death of Chriſt, and complete ſalvation in eternal Glory, notwithſtanding all our paſt ſins, however multiplied, or aggravated, they may have been. And how loſt muſt we be to all ingenuity and ſenſe of gratitude, if, by ſuch conſiderations, that "godly ſorrow" for ſin is not produced in us, which is accompained with "repentance unto life, never to be repented of"? Many, without all doubt, in apoſtolic days, and in every age ſince, by means of what has been ſuggeſted to their minds at the table of the Lord, and impreſſ'd on them by his Spirit, have been turned from viſible chriſtians only, to thoſe that are chriſtians in the real temper of their hearts. And what has been may be again. The ordinance of the ſupper is admirably well adapted to promote the edification of all that come to it in the ſerious exerciſe of faith, though their faith, at preſent, ſhould not be ſuch as will argue their being "born from above".——

AND as to thoſe who are already partakers
of

of the grace of God in truth, their is nothing in christianity better suited to help forward their growth in the divine life, than their attendance at the sacramental supper in a serious, devout and considerate manner. It is by the dying love of Christ, duly impressed on the mind by the Holy Ghost, that holy dispositions are both begun, maintained, increased, and perfected in the Soul. And what more effectual means could have been devised to awaken in us a sense of this love of Christ, and keep it in a vigorous lively state, than our partaking of that bread and wine which are instituted symbols of his body broken, and blood shed, for our pardon and salvation? If, in the exercise of faith, we employ our thoughts on those amazing objects that are here offered to contemplation, it must tend, in the strongest manner, to soften our hearts, inflame our affections, strengthen our graces, and establish our minds in all christian virtue; especially, as we may here expect the presence of Christ with us, by his Spirit, to guide our thoughts, assist our meditations, govern our views, encourage our hopes, comfort our hearts, and confirm in us the principles of goodness. Perhaps, the blessed Jesus is never more present with the true christian, to the purposes of spiritual light, love, joy and increase of holiness, than when he is at his table in a right frame of soul. I doubt not, there are those now present who can speak of special manifestations of their Savior at this ordinance, enlarging their views of the divine glory, invigorating their graces, and strengthening their feeble minds, so as that they have been able to run in the christian race, and not be weary; to walk and not faint.——

So that if we have any concern for the welfare of our souls; if we desire they should be possessed of the grace of God, or improved and established in it, we must needs think ourselves obliged to celebrate the memorial of Christ's dying love; as this is an instituted mean so powerfully fitted to produce these good effects.

It is, I am ready to think very much owing to the neglect of the Lord's Supper, that there is so little religion to be seen among us. While christians, so called, do generally, and allowedly express, in their practice, a disregard to their duty in this instance, it is no more than may be expected, that they should neglect it in another, and so on until they are got into an habit of indifference to all religion. It is likewise very much owing to the neglect of this ordinance, or a careless flighty manner of attending

attending on it, that there are so many spiritually poor, weak christians among us. No wonder persons should continue " babes in Christ", if they do not use this mean of growth, or, if they use it, do it in an overtly superficial manner.—It is owing to this same cause also, in a great measure, that there are so many christians, who conflict with doubts and fears, being strangers to that comfortable hope towards God without which there can be no true enjoyment of life ; and how should it be otherwise, if they will not wait upon Christ, in this way of his appointment, for those manifestations of his love which shall scatter their fears, and set their minds at rest ? It may be justly questioned, whether religion will ever flourish among us, until this institution of Christ is more generally attended, and with due care and consideration.

I shall subjoin here still further to excite our regard to the sacramental supper, that it is a visible mark, sign, or badge of the christian profession. The wisdom of God has always seen fit, under all the dispensations of his kingdom, to appoint some sacred visible rite, as a distinguishing mark pointing out his professing people. Circumcision was the instituted rite of distinction, to the seed of
Abraham

Abraham after the flesh. In addition hereto, the passover, under the law, was appointed, among other ends, to be a sign between God, and the nation of the Jews, that is, a public solemn rite by which they might be known to be his people, in distinction from the other nations of the earth. And of such importance were these instituted rites, in the esteem of God, that the despisers of them were peremptorily ordered by his authority to "be cut off from his people"; as not having their proper mark, and therefore no right to their advantages. Christianity also has its distinguishing rites. Meeting together for "supplications, prayers, intercessions, and giving of thanks," and the like public exercises of piety, are not peculiar to the religion of Jesus, but common to every other. Baptism, and the Lord's-Supper, are the sacred visible rites by which Christ would have his disciples and followers known to be such in distinction from the rest of the world. By baptism, which can be received but once, agreably to the mind of our Savior, they are initiated disciples; but it is principally by celebrating the Lord's-Supper, and doing it frequently in a stated course, that they are distinguished as his followers. By this they were known as such in the days of the apostles.

Their

Their aſſembling together to "break bread" was their appropriate character, and pointed them out as the diſciples of Chriſt. And ſo it ought to be now. We ſhould be known to be chriſtians by having communion in the emblems of Chriſt's body and blood. A crucified Chriſt is the true baſis of the religion of Jeſus, in diſtinction from every other; and the public ſolemn celebration of him in this character, in the way he has appointed, is the proper diſtinctive mark of our profeſſion as his diſciples. By this we "glory in the croſs of Chriſt", proclaiming our adherance to him, and that we have no hope towards God but through him. But if we are neglecters of the Lord's-Supper, we declare virtually, and in reality of ſenſe, that we are aſhamed of the proper chriſtian badge. And what ever elſe we do in religion, we leave that undone which is the inſtituted viſible mark to diſtinguiſh us as Chriſt's diſciples.

I HAVE now ſaid all that I intended in illuſtration of the bonds we are under to "break bread" as Chriſt has commanded.

LET what has been offered, be ſeriouſly reflected on by thoſe who have made it their practice to treat the table of the Lord with neglect

neglect, not to say constructive contempt. You have violated the strongest bonds, and must be convinced of it, if you will but consider. Is not the supper of the Lord a plain institution of the gospel? Has not Jesus Christ peremptorily said "do this in remembrance of me"? Can you call in question the truth of this command? Have you not as good reason to believe, that he has instituted the sacramental supper, as baptism, or the duty of attending to the word preached? And will you notwithstanding pay no regard to this gospel ordinance? Is he not the constituted sovereign in the kingdom of grace? Do you not call him Master and Lord? And is he not your Savior, as well as Lawgiver and Judge? Has he not died a sacrifice to atone for your sins? Have you any hope of the pardoning mercy of God, but through the merit of his blood, that blood of his, this institution is a memorial of. And will you, in opposition to all these constraining motives, go on in the neglect of it? God forbid that you should any longer disregard the authority of his Son Jesus Christ, and betray ingratitude to him for his astonishing love, by taking no practical notice of his dying request to his disciples and followers.

SERMON.

SERMON II.

Acts. II. 42.

"*And they continued steadfastly—in breaking of Bread*"

I HAVE already taken occasion, from these words, to lay before you, in a plain and faithful manner, the obligations christians are under to "break bread" in obedience to Christ, and in commemoration of his dying love to sinners.

WHAT I now propose is, a serious address, relative to the subject we have been upon, to the following classes of persons. To the securely

curely wicked; to the careless and indifferent; to those who neglect the Lord's-Supper, though it is their care to observe the other institutions of christianity; to those who call in question the perpetuity of the command to " break and eat bread" at the sacramental table; and, finally, to those who are sensible of their duty in this regard, and would gladly attend it, but that they are hindred by various doubts, fears, and spiritual difficulties.

By thus methodising this address, it will obviously and naturally fall in my way to consider the sacramental neglect in every point of view, and to offer thereupon what may be thought proper; not leaving untouched any objection, scruple, fear, or perplexity, however minute, any have mentioned, within my knowledge, in excuse of themselves. It has been my purpose, for some, considering the great and general, and, I may say, scandalous disregard that is practically shewn to as plain a duty as any in the religion of Jesus Christ, to be particular and thorough in an attempt of this nature; and if, in prosecution of it, several discourses should be found necessary, the importance of what may be delivered will render an apology needless: You will the rather give the more earnest and diligent attention to what may be discoursed. This may be expected

pected of those, at least, whose minds are in anxiety respecting their attendance at the gospel supper.

I am, in the first place, to address a few words to the securely wicked, those who lead a vicious and ungodly life, love the ways of sin, and walk in them, not perceiving within themselves an inclination to cease from doing evil, but a disposition and resolution rather to go on in the practice of iniquity. Would to God it were an abuse of christians, so called, to suppose there were any among them of this character. But it is a fact too glarringly evident to admit of a denial. To such I would say,

It is not expected of you, nor indeed desired, that you would, in your present temper of mind, come to the table of the Lord. It would be a prophanation of that which is sacred for persons of your character to partake of the symbols of Christ's body and blood; and should you attend any other service of piety, it would be only for fashion's sake, and in hypocrisy. You are the wicked ones of whom it is declared, in the sacred books, that " their prayers are an abomination to the Lord". You are the sinners, of whom the holy God makes that demand, " when ye come to appear

pear before me, who hath required this at your hands"? You are the persons, as though pointed out by name, to them he applies, in that most solemn language, "what hast thou to do, that thou shouldest take my covenant into thy mouth"? But remember, though the wicked state you are allowedly in is a good reason, why you should not dare to partake of the Lord's Supper, it is, at the same time, a reason that will render you speechless, when you are called to stand before the bar of the coming judgment. Far from cancelling your obligations to this duty, it heinously aggravates your guilt in the neglect of it. You are the more inexcusible, as your being altogether unfitted for this, or indeed any other sacred performance, is owing to your vicious indulgences as willing servants of corruption. If any of you, my hearers, are conscious to yourselves, that you are the sinners here described, be assured, your state, religiously speaking, is lamentably sad. You will only mock God, should you pretend to draw nigh to him in the exercises of piety. And yet, your guilt in not doing this, instead of being lessened by your being thus sinful, will be greatly inhanced. Is then the condition you are in a safe one? Can you be easie in it? The
Lord

Lord take pity on you! Unlefs you are awakened to attention, and brought to a fight of your finfulnefs and danger, you are undone for the future world. This is the firft thing neceffary in order to your recovery. If it fhall pleafe the father of mercies, and God of all grace, to alarm your fears, roufe your confciences, and put you upon feeking to him in real earneft to compafionate your cafe, there will be hope concerning you. You may, if he fhould gracioufly do this, with propriety ufe the appointed means in order to a " deliverance from the bondage of corruption into the glorious liberty of the fons of God"; and you may do it, humbly hopeing for fuccefs, through him who has been the propitiation for the fins of men.

THE carelefs and indifferent are nextly to be applied to; by whom I intend, not thofe who have no fenfe of religion, and pay no regard at all to it, making fin, in one fhape or another, their habitual allowed practice: Thefe are not the perfons I have here in view; but thofe, who, though they may have fome perceptions of the bonds of God that are upon them, are yet the fubjects of them in a tranfient way only, and this in a low feeble degree, fo as that they have no

power

power to form their temper, or thoroughly touch their conscience. Their proper character is, not that they are totally thoughtless, but insufficiently so; not that they are altogether unconcerned about the affairs of their souls and another world, but their concern about these infinitely important matters is light and inconsiderable; not that they never have any religious motions working in them, but they are weak, fluctuating and ineffectual; insomuch that they can indulge to carelesness in regard of the duties of piety, and yet keep their minds in ease and peace; yea, they can live in the habitual neglect of them, or, which is as bad, a meer formal, customary performance of them, and perceive no uneasiness on this account. Many there are, and among those too who would take it ill not to be called christians, whose just character has been here delineated, To such it may not be amiss to say,

YOUR great unhappiness is, that religion has taken no fast hold of your hearts. You are not only strangers to the power of godliness but to that state of mind that is only introductory to it. It is seldom, if ever, that persons take up the practice of religion with engagedness of heart, until they have
first

first had excited in them such perceptions of God, and their obligations to him, as are incompatible with that indifferency of spirit which distinguishes the persons to whom I am now speaking. Instead therefore of being christians in truth, you have not as yet attained to that serious state of mind, that sense of God, of sin and holiness, which are common to those who are but just entering upon the business of religion in good earnest.

The proper advice to you is, to endeavour, in all sutable ways, to get awakened in you a becoming concern about the infinitely interesting affairs of your souls, and everlasting salvation. Without this, if you do any thing in religion it will be a lip-service only. If you " honor God with your mouths, your hearts will be far from him". And, perhaps, duty thus performed, had as well been omitted. Be sure, the supper of the Lord should not be attended in this sleighty, superficial, not to say hypocritical manner. It would be a dishonor to the memory of Christ's dying love, and of no service to those, who in this heedless way, should join in the celebration of it. Not that persons will be discharged from guilt, if they neglect duty in general, or the duty of partaking of the
                                                sacramental

sacramental supper in particular, on account of the inconsiderate unconcerned frame of mind they are habitually in. This would be to suppose, that one sin might be an excuse for another, than which nothing is more palpably absurd. Your sin, in neglecting your duty, will be the more heinous in God's sight, as taking rise from so bad a cause as that of a thoughtless state of soul, rendering you unmeet for the performance of it.

The first thing therefore proper for you is, to pay regard to that inspired direction, "consider, and shew yourselves men". Make use of the power of reflection you are endowed with, and is your distinguishing glory as men, reasonable creatures. And be much in the exercise of it; taking off your thoughts from the world, its vanities, gayities, amusements, riches and pleasures, and employing them on those spiritual objects that will tend to soften your hearts, warm your affections, and animate your resolutions and endeavors. Without this care, it will be impossible, humanly speaking, but that you should remain destitute of any lively sense of God and religion, and indifferent to things of a spiritual nature. It is by meditation, serious, frequent, devout meditation, that the mind is impressed

fed, and a concern about the "one thing needful" at first excited, and afterwards maintained and cherished. And you can be at no loss for objects, which, if solemnly meditated on, in the exercise of a rational faith only, would mightily tend to awaken your consciences, and promote in you a becoming sollicitude about your highest interest. Think of God, your relation to him, your dependance on him, and the inviolable obligations you are under to love, honor and serve him. Think on Christ, what he has done, and suffered, and is now doing at God's right hand in heaven for your salvation; what he expects from you in return for all this goodness, and what you may expect from him, if you treat it with ingratitude and base neglect. Think on the coming of the Lord Jesus Christ a second time, his coming in the glory of his father, and in his own glory, with the holy angels, to judge the world in righteousness, when you shall stand before his tribunal, and, if you have not been careful to approve yourselves his faithful and obedient servants, shall receive that sentence from his mouth, "depart from me, ye cursed, into the fire prepared for the devil and his angels". Oh amazing object of contemplation! What can be more powerfully adapted to move your fear, awaken your concern, and engage your earnest endeavours, that you may be found of your Judge, in that day, among those, to whom he will say, " come ye blessed of my father, inherit the kingdom prepared for you from the foundation of the world". Can you make present to your view, in serious contemplation, this awful day of the Son of God, and not be concerned that you may then hold up your heads with joy? Can it be supposed, that you have faith, so much as a common faith, in this most serious and important truth, unless, when you employ your thoughts on it, your indifferency to religion, your carelessness in reference to the duties of it, receive some solemn check, unless they no longer operate as your habitual governing temper? If you are, any of you, to such a degree thoughtless, and unconcerned, as that you will not reflect on these interesting objects of revelation, or are able to think of them with so little attention as not to be moved by them, you are in an unhappy condition. The "god of this world" has blinded your eyes, and you will remain in this spiritually hazardous state, until you are

brought

brought to confider, and fo to confider as to be hereby thoroughly roufed. And whenever this fhall come to be your cafe, you will attend the duties of piety, and you will do it from the heart, and not in hypocrify; in real good earneft, and not as a matter of form: And by thus attending on the inftituted means of grace, you may hope, under the concurring influence of the Spirit of God, to be trained up to a " meetnefs for the inheritance of the fanctified by faith in Jefus Chrift".

ANOTHER fort of perfons to be fpoken to are thofe, who, inftead of indulging to vice, are blamelefs in their lives. Their turn of mind is ferious and confiderate. They make it their practice to perform the other duties of religion, though not that of remembring Chrift at his table. It is their care to " pray to their father, who feeth in fecret"; the " morning and evening facrifice" is daily going up as " incenfe" from their houfes; they come to the " fanctuary" at the ftated times for worfhip, and join with God's people in the public offices of religion, the celebration of the facrament only excepted. Nor is this a meer cuftomary bufinefs, a matter of form only. They efteem

it

it their duty, are confciencious in the doing
it, and it would occafion uneafy reflections
on themfelves, fhould they needlefsly neglect it. Some there are, it may be hoped
a good number, of whom this is the juft
character. To fuch I would fay,

It is to your commendation, that you attend thefe duties of piety. But what good account can you give of your leaving the other
undone? Has Chrift, the law-giver, King, and
Judge of his Church, diftinguifhed between
the facramental inftitution, and the other duties of religion, excufing your obfervance of
the former, if you practically regard the latter? Has he not rather peremptorily required
your obedience to them all? Is it not as truly
his will, explicitly and folemnly publifhed, that
you fhould celebrate the memorial of his dying love, as that you fhould pray to God, or
take heed to the word of doctrine or exhor-
tation? And if it is proper you fhould obey
him in thefe inftances, why not in the other?
Is not his authority the fame in all thefe requirements? And will you do juft honor to it,
if, while you are obedient in fome inftances,
you are difobedient in another? Your attending the other exercifes of piety will not be accounted another day a good reafon for the
neglect

neglect of this. It will rather be esteemed an evidence of deficiency in your regard to the government of him who is your professed Master and Lord. It is not enough my brethren, that you give your attendance on prayer, and the word preached. You are as much obliged to " break bread" at the Lord's-Supper. You may no more omit the one than the other. They are equally your duty: or, should there be any difference, your obligations to pay a becoming respect to the sacramental institution are the strongest, and should make you more especially careful not to treat it with neglect. " This do in remembrance of me," is the dying command of your Savior, as well as Lord; and it is a command that enjoins your remembrance of the greatest love of the best friend. You are bound therefore in gratitude as well as duty to yield a ready chearful obedience to it. It is strange that any, who have upon their minds a serious sense of religion, and are hereupon careful in other respects to do the duties of it, should yet live month after month, and year after year, in the omission of this. It is more strange still, that they should be uneasy in their minds, should they neglect those duties, while yet they can go on in the neglect of this, and meet with little

or

or no disturbance from the resentments of conscience. How far this constant omission of duty, in so important an article, may consist with the truth of grace, belongs only to Christ to determine. Unhappy mistakes, scruples, and fears, relative to the Lord's-Supper, (which may come under consideration in their proper place) will doubtless extenuate their fault: But when our Lord has so clearly and fully made known his will upon this head, it is difficult to conceive of any thing that will be sufficient to discharge us from the guilt of ingratitude to our Saviour, and the want of a due regard to his authority, as our rightful sovereign, while we make it our practice to turn away from his table.

Another class of persons still may be applied to; and they are those who pretend that the supper of the Lord is a temporary appointment, designed for the apostolic days only, confined to them, and ceasing with them as to its use and obligation.

To such it must be said, their notion of this matter is glaringly a mistaken one. And it may with all freedom be thus spoken of, as the apostle Paul has expressly assured us, and upon previous instruction immediately from Jesus Christ himself, that the "Lord's death"

death" is to to be "shewed forth until he comes", 1 Cor. 11. 26. What is the apostle's meaning in the phrase he here uses, " until he comes"? Surely he cannot intend the coming of Christ by his Spirit ; for, in this sense, he had already come, and remarkably too on the day of penticost, when the Spirit was poured out upon the apostles in miraculous gifts and powers. Neither could he mean the coming of Christ to destroy Jerusalem. This event, however awful in its effects upon the jewish nation, had no immediate reference to the gentile church at Corinth. There would be no pertinency in the apostle's arguing with this church, in relation to their observance of the Lord's Supper, upon such an interpretation of his words, And there is no other "coming of Christ", spoken of in scripture, but his "coming" at the end of the world, "in the glory of his father, with his holy angels" when a period will be put to the administration of God's kingdom in its present form. So that, if we may depend upon the apostle Paul, the sacramental supper was not a temporary institution, but a perpetual one ; not designed for the primitive christians in the first age only, but for all christians in all ages to the end of the world. For the death of

Christ

Chriſt is to be "ſhewed forth until he come", and he will not come until the "myſtery of God is finiſhed", and "time ſhall be no more".

Besides, the paſſages of ſcripture which treat of this ordinance injoin the obſervation of it, and point out the manner in which it ſhould be done, were wrote, in the divine intention, for the uſe and benefit of chriſtians throughout all ages, and not for their's only to whom they were immediately directed. There is no chriſtian, in any part, or age of the world, but is as truly concerned, as the chriſtians at Corinth, in that apoſtolic advice, 1 Cor. 11. 25, "let a man examine himſelf, and ſo let him eat of this bread, and drink of this cup".

The end alſo propoſed by our Savior, in the appointment of this ſacred rite, is a clear and full proof that it is of perpetual continuance, and obligatory upon chriſtians in all ages until the end of time. Whatever other ends might be in the view of our Savior, this was certainly one, that the remembrance of his death, by a figurative repreſentation of it, publicly recogniſed, might not be forgot, but kept ſtrong and vigorous in the minds of chriſtians. And if it was at all needful, in this way, to keep alive the memory of Chriſt's death

death, it was surely as needful in after ages, as in the first days of christianity. There was indeed less occasion for this appointment at first, because less danger of a forgetfulness of Christ's death. In succeeding ages, there would be increased danger lest he should be forgot. And that the remembrance of him might be preserved, continued, and upheld, he instituted this memorial. So that it was more especially designed for after ages, who, by this emblematical representation of him as crucified and slain, might have the reality of this fact, the great foundation of the christian scheme, lively in their minds. The longer it is since Christ's body was broken, and his blood shed, the more need there is of this memorial of it; and there will be need of it, and continually increasing need, until time shall be no more. His death therefore must be " shewed forth," in the way of divine appointment, " until he comes." The obligation to this, instead of being lessened, grows stronger, in proportion to the distance from the time of his death, as a sacrifice for sin.

It may be added to what has been said, that the ordinance of the supper is as suitably and powerfully adapted, in its nature, to be

beneficial

beneficial to chriſtians in all ages, as in the firſt days of the goſpel. It offers the ſame occaſion, by figurative, yet expreſſive ſigns, for contemplation on the moſt affecting and intereſting objects. It has the ſame virtue it ever had, and will retain it, in all future time, to awaken the attention, to excite affection, to melt the heart, and, in a word, to beget and confirm every real principle of goodneſs in the ſoul. It has all along been productive of theſe happy effects, it ſtill produces them, and is equally fitted to anſwer ſo valuable an end in time yet to come. Why then ſhould the uſe of this ordinance be diſcontinued ? Why ſhould it be thought a temporary one ? There is the ſame reaſon for its being a perpetual appointment, as for its being an appointment at all. It is equally fitted for the uſe of chriſtians at all times, and may be, unleſs from their own faultineſs, of like benefit to them. It would therefore be a diſhonour to Chriſt, by putting an undue limitation on his goodneſs to his church, to ſuppoſe, that he ſhould deſign ſo uſeful, ſo beneficial an inſtitution for his diſciples only in the firſt age, when they all, in all ages, might reap the ſame ſpiritual profit therefrom.

THERE

There is yet another sort of persons to be spoken to, the fearful and scrupulous, those who labor of doubts, and have their minds perplexed with difficulties. But, as my design here is, to be particular and full, that I may, if possible remove out of the minds of this kind of persons all scruples and fears, that they may come with comfort and pleasure to the Lord's table, I must defer what I have to say, until some further opportunity, if God shall please to grant it.

In the meam time, let us be thankful to Christ, that, before he left the world, he was so concerned for the good of those, who should be his disciples, in all after-time, as to institute the supper, a mean happily calculated to promote their edification in faith, love, and all christian graces. We should not be so insensible of our own spiritual profit, or of the bonds we are under of gratitude to Christ, as to treat this appointment of his love with neglect.

Let us also, from what has been said, be confirmed in our belief of the perpetuity of
the

the christian church. If the ordinance of the supper was intended for a perpetually continuing one, there will be a perpetual succession of christians to attend the celebration of it. As surely as Christ designed, that his death should be "shewed forth until he comes", so surely will he have a church on earth to do this, until the commencement of this signal time. There may be a failure, a total failure, of christians in name, as well as reality, in this and the other nation; while yet he may have a church in the world; And he will perpetually have a succession of disciples to recognise the memory of his death, in the manner he has appointed, who, by this, among other means, shall be built up in faith and comfort, until the consummation of all things: Nor shall the combined powers of earth and hell be able to prevent it.

LET us likewise be firmly persuaded, that those are under the influence of delusive error, who imagine they are above the use of the ordinance of the supper. Whatever measures of the Spirit such may pretend to above others, they are not under his guidance in this matter. None among the followers of Christ ever yet

yet attained to such perfection in this life, as to have no need of this institution of his, which will remain in force "until he comes". And is Christ already come, a second time? Have we yet seen the described signs of his appearing? We must wait for this, before the Lord's-Supper may be put by, as having continued its appointed time.

In fine, we may properly take occasion, from what has been said, to look and long for the happy privileges of heaven. There will, in that blessed place, be no use for those means, and helps, that are necessary in this present state. Even the ordinance of the supper will be no more celebrated after the coming of Christ. In consequence of this, there will be an intire change in the manner of administration in God's kingdom. We "see now as through a glass darkly"; but then we shall "see face to face, and know even as we are known". We now enjoy God in the use of ordinances; we shall then enjoy him in a more immediate way. We are now, after our highest attainments, in the best use of appointed means, poor, weak, imperfect creatures; we shall then be advanced to such a noble degree of perfection

fection, as to be able to converse with God, and Jesus Christ, in another and far more exalted manner, so as to be completely, uninterruptedly and eternally happy. God grant it may be the portion of us all, through Jesus Christ, to him be glory.

A M E N.

SERMON

SERMON III.

Acts. II. 42.

" And they continued steadfastly—in breaking " of Bread"

EVERAL classes of persons have been applied to, from these words, in relation to an attendance on the sacramental " breaking of bread."

It remains to speak to the scrupulous and fearful, those who are kept from this ordinance, not from a thoughtless, careless temper of mind, much less an indulged contempt of the authority of Jesus Christ; but by reason of doubts

and

and difficulties that lie in the way of their obedience to it. These are many and various. It shall be my endeavour to take due notice of them all, so far as I am acquainted with them; not studying to range them in any nice order, but rather bringing them to view as they may occur to mind.

The first ground of fear I would mention is, the apprehension many have of some peculiar kind of sanctity in this ordinance. They imagine it to be holy in a sense different from that, in which the other institutions of christianity are holy; and are therefore scrupulous, as to their attendance on it; while yet they can, without difficulty, attend the other appointments of gospel worship.

In order to remove away this ground of fear, I would not say a word to lessen, in the minds of any, a just sense of that holy reverence with which they should always approach to the table of the Lord; but it may, at the same time, be proper to put persons upon due care to guard themselves against superstitious notions, respecting the holiness of the bread and wine, of which they eat and drink at the sacramental supper. These, it may be, are the source, at bottom, of the scrupulous fear I am now considering. It takes rise,

not

not from juſt ſentiments of the nature, deſign, or tendency of the Lord's-Supper; but from a mind tinctured with ſuperſtitious awe and veneration. This is certainly the truth, if we imagine, that holineſs, in any degree, is tranſmitted into the bread and wine by their conſecration to the ſacramental uſe. Many, I have reaſon to think, entertain this thought of the matter. But it is intirely a falſe notion. The bread and wine are no otherwiſe holy, after their conſecration, than as they are ſeparated to an holy uſe, and in this way become capable of being improved to promote holineſs in us. The ordinance of the ſupper is not therefore holy in a ſenſe any way different from that, in which the other inſtitutions of religion are holy. They are all holy, as intended, and adapted, to make men holy, and ought practically to be regarded without diſtinction, or diſcrimination. Surely we cannot, upon juſt and ſolid grounds, ſcruple the uſe of the ſacramental inſtitution, meerly becauſe it is an holy one, while we freely uſe the other inſtitutions of religion, all which are holy alſo, and in the ſame ſenſe preciſely too, in which the ſupper of the Lord is holy. Yes, if the " breaking and eating of bread" at the ſacramental-table, ſhould be esteemed, even, more holy than any other acts of instituted religion, it would be so far from being a good reason why we should not do this duty, that it ought rather more powerfully to constrain us to it. For why should the Lord's Supper be esteemed more holy, than the other appointments of christian worship? It can justly be so in no sense but this, its being better fitted to promote holiness in us. And shall any, who profess a serious sense of God, and the obligations of religion, scruple the use of the sacramental institution for this reason. They should rather look upon themselves so much the more bound to a faithful, constant, consciencious observance of it: Yea, so far as they have it in their view to become holy, or to be made more so, by their attendance on the institutions of the gospel, they should be particular in their care not to neglect this, as it is the most powerfully suited to promote this good end.

I shall subjoin here a remark not unworthy of notice. It is this. Christians, for many ages, by means of the popish doctrine of transubstantiation, entertained superstitious, not to say idolotrous, notions of the sacramental bread and wine; supposing that they were converted into the real body and blood of Jesus

Jesus Christ. And though the doctrine, from whence these false notions took rise, has, since the reformation, been discarded by those who are called protestants; yet may it be feared, whether some tincture of the old leaven does not still remain in the minds of too many. Thus much, at least, may naturally and reasonably be supposed, that christians, upon seperating from the church of Rome, retained so much of their former superstition, as to place too great a difference between the sacramental supper, and other religious duties. For this reason they abstained from an attendance at the Lord's table, while they observed the other institutions of gospel-worship; and, by this means, there might be propagated, in the minds of many, from that day to this, such a notion of the peculiar holiness of this ordinance, as that they are hardly brought to pay a practical regard to it. Whether this is a just account of the matter, or not, it is certain, however it comes about, that many serious good people entertain mistaken apprehensions of the holiness of this ordinance; otherwise they would not be induced, from such apprehensions, to abstain from the use of it. It can, with propriety and truth, be called an holy ordinance, only as it was

appointed

appointed to an holy purpose and use, and as it is a proper and powerful means to make the obervers of it holy, according to man's measure, as God is holy. And surely, as has been said, this is a good reason why we should join in celebrating the Lord's-Supper; but a very bad one why we should neglect to do so. Surely, the reasoning cannot be just, the supper of the Lord is holy, as being a divine appointment happily calculated to make men holy; I ought not therefore to be a partaker at it, I may not approach to it. How glaringly absurd is such arguing as this! Whereas, the arguing, on the contrary, is strictly right, and strongly conclusive, the sacramental-supper was instituted with a view to make men holy, and is powerfully fitted to such a purpose, it is therefore my wisdom, my interest, my duty, to be a partaker at it; and the more holy it is, on account of its tendency and suitableness to make men holy, the more wise I shall approve my self, the more I shall consult my truest interest, the more will my conduct agree with what is right, proper and fit, while I am instant, steady and diligent in paying a religious regard, in my practice, to this sacred institution of the gospel.

So that, upon the whole, the fear any serious

ous, thoughtful, chriſtians may have on their minds, relative to their participation of the Lord's-Supper, as taking riſe from the holineſs of this rite of goſpel worſhip, has really no juſt foundation. You ſhould rather fear, my brethren, leſt you ſhould diſhonour Chriſt by neglecting a divinely appointed mean, and the moſt wiſely and powerfully adapted one, in order to your being holy, while you neglect to give your preſence at the ſacramental table. You cannot indeed expect to be holy, to be ſure not eminently ſo, while you difuſe this ſpecial and powerful means in order to it.

ANOTHER thing that keeps ſome from the goſpel-ſupper is, a fear leſt they ſhould not live as may be reaſonably expected of thoſe, who "eat and drink in Chriſt's preſence"; they think, and with great truth and juſtice, that all, who come to the table of the Lord, ſhould adorn their character, as the diſciples of Chriſt, by a well-ordered converſation; cauſing their "light to ſhine before others, that, ſeeing their good works, they may glorify their father in heaven". But they fear, leſt they ſhould not "walk worthy of the Lord". Others, they obſerve, are too frequently faulty, in this regard, to

the

the reproach of Christ, and scandal of his holy religion; and, fearing lest they should be thus faulty, they are restrained from coming to the supper of their Lord; imagining they had better be non-attendants at it, than run the hazard of this guilt.

To such I would say, your fear is just, but does not operate in a right manner. You ought to be "jealous over yourselves with a godly jealousy"; encouraging a fear, lest you should act an unworthy part, and dishonor your Savior, by a walk in the world unbecoming the gospel, and the highest profession of its bonds on you. But then, it should be your care to govern the influence of this fear, so as that, instead of being an hindrance to you in duty, it may rather invigorate your endeavours to put it fully in practice. Your fear is, lest you should not honor your profession; and it is a fear that well becomes all the professors of christianity. But what ought, in true reason, to be its operation? Surely, not to restrain you from making a profession. This would be a counter-action to its proper design, and genuine tendency. It should rather put you upon greater watchfulness, and circumspection. It should quicken your zeal, and make you more earnest and resolute

resolute in your endeavours, under the blessing of God, to behave in the world with that sobriety, purity, and righteousness, which become those who sit down as guests at the table of Christ.

It is observable, the holy apostles were afraid lest those who professed faith in Christ, and were admitted to break that bread, which is the instituted memorial of his broken body, should be unmindful of the bonds of God that were upon them, and live in a manner unworthy of their character as the disciples of Christ. But how did their fear operate? Not by advising men to forbear professing Christ, or eating and drinking with him at his table. Not a word of this tendency is to be met with, any where in the new-testament. But, in consequence of this fear, their exhortations were, to "hold fast the profession of their faith"; to "take heed, watch and pray"; to be diligent and laborious, that their walk in the world might be "worthy of that God who had called them into his kingdom". And this should be the influence of the fear I am now speaking of; and this will be its influence, if duly regulated. It will not restrain any from remembering the dying love of their Lord, in the way of his appointment

ment, but rather firſt urge them to it, and then make them earneſt and faithful in their endeavours to behave, in all reſpects, as thoſe ought to do, who are admitted to ſo near communion with their Savior and Lord.

I SHALL not think it either impertinent, or unſeaſonable, if I add a word here to thoſe communicants, who, by their unguarded, miſbecoming conduct, are the occaſion of that fear in the minds of many, which reſtrains them from joining with their chriſtian brethren in partaking of the ſymbols of Chriſt's body and blood. It is too glaring a truth to be diſowned, that, among the gueſts at the ſacramental ſupper, there are too many who live as though they were inſenſible of the bonds they are under to "order their converſation in ſimplicity and godly ſincerity, not by fleſhly wiſdom, but by the grace of God" Inſtead of being bright examples of thoſe virtues that are ornamental to chriſtians, and honorary to the religion they profeſs, they are too much conformed to this evil world, and appear too like the men of it. The plain truth is, the unhallowed lives of thoſe, who ſit down at the Lord's table, has been a ſtumbling-block to many ſerious, conſiderate, well-diſpoſed perſons. Far from exciting them to glorify God by the luſtre
of

of these graces, they have rather, by their unchristian behavior of themselves, made them afraid of professing Christ, lest they also should be a reproach both to him, and his holy religion. This, my brethren, is utterly a fault. We who "call Christ Lord, Lord, and eat and drink in his presence", should above all things make it our care to "walk worthy of him unto all pleasing". We should keep at the utmost distance from every thing vicious and immoral; and not only so, but should be found in the practice of all the virtues that are amiable and praise-worthy. We should be grave and modest in our behaviour, sober and useful in our discourse, diligent and faithful in our respective callings, just and honest in our dealings. We should daily live in the exercise of meekness, patience, faith, temperance, humility. We should be courteous in our converse, gentle, kind, peceable and obliging in our carriage; and, as we have opportunity, should, according to our ability, " do good to all men, especially to the houshold of faith". In a word, "whatsoever things are true, whatsoever things are honest, whatsoever things are just, whatsoever things are pure, whatsoever things are lovely, whatsoever things are of good report, if there be any virtue, and if there be any praise, we should think on these things", so think on them as to exhibit in our lives a conspicuous example of them: So shall we honour ourselves, and reflect glory on our Saviour and master Jesus Christ; and, instead of deterring others from the table of the Lord, we shall, in the most constraining manner, invite and urge them to be present as guests at it.—But to leave this digression, if any should please so to call it.

Another difficulty still in the way of some is a fear, lest, if they should be overcome to commit sin after they have ate and drank at the sacramental supper, they should never obtain forgiveness. This may not be a difficulty that has perplexed the minds of many; but some, I have reason to think, are kept from the Lord's-Supper through fear, taking rise from this view of the matter.

But it is a fear altogether imaginary. Nothing in all the Bible gives the least countenance to it. Far from this, we are assured, in that sacred book, "that if any man should sin", be it before, or after, his breaking and eating bread at the sacramental table, "we have an advocate with the father, Jesus the righteous, who has been the propitiation for our sins". And this Jesus, who died a sacrifice for transgression, has himself most preremptorily

rily declared, in terms too plain and exprefs to be eafily mifunderftood, that but one fin, the fin of blafpheming the holy Ghoft, is excepted out of the gofpel-grant of pardoning mercy. So that whatever our fins may have been, and whenfoever committed, whether before or after a profeffion of Chrift, and eating and drinking in his prefence, they come within the reach of offered, and promifed forgivenefs, and fhall certainly, upon our repentance, be pardoned for the fake of Chrift, and on account of that atonement he has made for the fins of men.

It is true, fins that are committed after the higheft profeffion of love to Chrift, and fubjection to his authority, are aggravated in their guilt; but whatever aggravating circumftances attend them, they are not fuch as will obftruct the beftowment of God's mercy in the remiffion of them, in regard of thofe, who in the exercife of true repentance, repair to him for this bleffing. Thofe words of the apoftle Paul contain enough in them forever to fatisfy us of this, "where fin has abounded, grace does much more abound"; though we fhould take care we do not abufe this grace, by encouraging ourfelves to fin, that God's grace in the pardon of it may abound

towards

towards us. This would argue the bafeft ingratitude. Shall we be evil, becaufe God is good? God forbid!

It is true likewife, if any, after fuch ferious impreffions as have put them upon an attendance "on the word, breaking of bread, and prayer", relapfe into thoughtlefsnefs and fecurity, infomuch that they can "fin wilfully", and in an habitual courfe, "the latter end with them is worfe than the beginning"; the danger awfully great, left they fhould "fail of the grace of God" and be "not again renewed to repentance". But the cafe even of this kind of perfons is not without all hope. It is poffible they may be awakned to a juft fenfe of things, and be brought to that "repentance which is unto life, not to be repented of"; though their ftate, it muft be acknowledged, is hazardous; as they cannot be renewed by repentance, but with extreme difficulty.

The apoftle Paul fometimes fuppofes, that profeffors of religion, even thofe among them who have been admitted to the higheft privileges of God's vifible kingdom, may fhamefully backflide. And what does he fay hereupon? Does he put any upon neglecting gofpel inftitutions through fear, left they fhould afterwards

afterwards relapſe into ſin? Far from this, he adviſes them to be ſteady and perſevering in the uſe of them; and to take occaſion from fear of a relapſe, to be cautious and circumſpect, to look well to themſelves, to be upon their guard, and to hold out againſt all oppoſition in the way of well-doing, that, being faithful to the death, they may obtain the crown of eternal life. And this ſhould be the influence of our fear, reſpecting ſin after having ate and drank at the table of the Chriſt. Inſtead of keeping us from this duty, it ſhould keep us upon our guard, and make us the more watchful over our hearts and lives.

ANOTHER difficulty yet in the way of many to their attendance at the ſacramental ſupper is, a fear leſt they are not prepared for ſo ſacred an ordinance.

To this it might be ſufficient to ſay, the duty of this kind of perſons is ſo plain, as not to admit of diſpute. They ſhould inſtantly ſet about the work of preparation, and give themſelves no eaſe, until it is accompliſhed; and the rather, becauſe, if it is the real truth, that they are eſſentially wanting in a preparedneſs, in the frame of their minds, for an approach to the table of Chriſt, they can have

have no good hope towards God. They are unmeet for the kingdom of heaven, and shall not be admitted to sit down there, at the eternal supper of the lamb. And, surely, this is not a state to be continued in with peace and quiet of soul.

But, as this difficulty is the most common one, and keeps a great many from the sacramental table, I shall be more particular and distinct in offering what may be sufficient to remove it away.

You say, you fear whether you are prepared to eat bread and drink wine with Christ at his table; and your fear restrains you from attending this instance of duty.

Permit me to ask you, what do you mean by this preparation, you are afraid you are destitute of? This is an important question in the present case, and the true answer to it will make way for the removal of all the difficulty that is perplexing to you.

Do you mean, when you say you are not prepared for the sacrament, that your state in such, as that, if you attend this duty, it must be done with some mixture of frailty and imperfection? If this is
what

what you mean, you are to be plainly told, that you will never be able to attend the memorial of your Saviour's death in a manner perfectly freed from all mixture of sin. You will, as long as you live, continue frail imperfect creatures; and God has made no provision in the Gospel to prevent it. If therefore you imagine, you must not come to the sacrament, until you can attend there without any mixture of corruption, you must never come: And should others think as you do, neither would they come; the consequence of which would be, that the sacramental supper would have no guests to attend it; nor indeed ought it to have any. The real truth is, our Lord appointed the memorial of his death for poor, weak, imperfect, and sinful creatures, as the best of men always have been, and always will be to the end of the world. And if such may not remember the dying love of their Lord, in the way of his special appointment, it must never be done in in this world, and so never done at all. For good men, in the coming world, will be above the need, or use, of this, or any other instrumental mean, as being perfect

in

in their conformity to the image of Christ, as he is to the image of the invisible God.

Do you mean, when you say you are not prepared for the sacrament, that you have not as yet attained to a confirmed, well established state of goodness? Surely, this should be no bar in your way. It ought rather to be a motive powerfully constraining you to give your instant and constant attendance on this institution of the gospel. For it was appointed by Christ, the head of his church, as a wisely and suitably adapted, mean, among other things, to confirm the habits of grace, and make them well established principles of all virtuous, and christian good practice; and it is, by the use of this divinely appointed mean of grace, as well as by the word, that we are to grow, from the state of babes and children, to that of complete men in Christ. You will therefore, not only dishonour Christ, but wrong yourselves, if, from such a mistaken notion, you neglect your duty. The more weak and imperfect you are in goodness, the more reason you have for the use of this mean of grace. How can you use a more proper powerful method to grow up to the "fullnefs of Chrift". You would, if you were conftant, and confciencious in this near approach to God, and intimate communion with Chrift, be formed more and more to the temper of heaven, and a meetnefs for the imployments and injoyments of that bleffed world. Sin would continually grow weaker and weaker, and grace ftronger and ftronger. In a word, by thus commemorating the love of your Saviour, you would ufe a divinely appointed mean, to ftrengthen your pious refolutions, invigorate your virtuous principles, and animate your upright endeavours to grow in a likenefs to God, and Jefus Chrift, and every thing that is fpiritually good.

Do you mean when fay you are not prepared for the facrament, that you are ignorant of its nature, or of the manner in which you fhould attend at it; and, not having fufficient knowledge relative to this inftitution of religion, you fear you fhould do ill to come to it.

The anfwer here is eafie and fhort. If you are in earneft in fpeaking of this as a difficulty, and it is the real truth that you are thus ignorant, there is no need

need you should long continue so, and the fault will be your own if you do. You are favored with all advantages, in order to gain a sufficiency of knowledge, with reference to the sacrament. You have the bible in your hands, which records its institution, explains its nature and design, and directs as to the manner of attending at it. You have likewise, within your reach, a variety of valuable books, purposely wrote by the best of men, for your help in understanding the scripture upon this head. You may also repair, whenever you please, to christian friends and ministers, for all needed instruction. And if under the enjoyment of such advantages as these, you continue ignorant, the fault will be your own, and it will be inexcusably great. It will indeed be evident, that this difficulty, with which you excuse yourselves from coming to the sacrament, is a meer pretence. It will surely be so esteemed by your Saviour, who will also be your Judge in the great day of reckoning.

Do you mean, when you say you fear whether you are prepared for the sacrament, that your fear is, whether you are the

the subjects of the saving grace of God, and so think you had better stay away from this ordinance, until you are more free from doubt upon this head.

To SUCH, as it is my design more largely to consider this difficulty by itself in its proper place, I shall only say at present, It may be your fear, left you have not been partakers of the grace of God in truth, is a false one. You may, notwithstanding this fear, have " passed from death to life," and be known by Christ to be in the number of those who are HIS in the special and eminent sense. Many, among the true fearers of God, have lived, and died, under the prevailence of uncomfortable fears, respecting their spiritual state. It is therefore no sure argument, that you have not been formed to a likeness to God, in his moral glory, that you have no lively perceptions of it, but rather conflict with doubts and fears, left this should not be the truth of your case. And let me further say here, the most likely way you can take for the removal of your doubts and fears, is, to give your attendance instantly, and to continue it statedly, at the sacramental table.

What

What matter of wonder is it, you should be in doubt about the goodness of your state, while you habitually neglect your duty in as plain and evident an article, as any in all the bible? God may be displeased with this sin of yours, and "hide his face" from you. And what is also worthy of serious considerations while you neglect the sacrament, you neglect a mean of grace happily and powerfully suited to give you such views of the love of Christ, as may excite the exercise of love to him, in a degree enabling you to say, "Lord, thou knowest that I love thee." There are, among serious good christians, who can tell you, they have come away from the sacrament with a refreshing sense of their interest in the dying love of their Saviour, though they have gone to it in darkness and perplexity.

But let it be supposed, that you are not as yet in what the scripture calls a regenerate state. Is there nothing, at the sacramental table, that is fitted to beget in you the life of God, and true holiness? Have there never been instances of those, in whom the work of grace was begun
with

with power, by means of a crucified Chriſt, here exhibited to open view? And why may not you alſo be thus effectually wrought upon, under the influence of divine grace? There is nothing, my hearers, that can operate upon the human mind, in a way of means, to ſaving purpoſe, but what is held forth plainly, though by figurative ſigns, at the ſacramental table. And the truths here preached may as well have their operation while you are here, as at any other time, or in any other place.

I would not, by what I now ſay, be underſtood to encourage thoſe to come to the ordinance of the ſupper, who are thoughtleſs and unconcerned, inſenſible of ſin, and unreſolved as to putting themſelves under the guidance, inſtruction, and government of Chriſt. But this is far from being the caſe of thoſe I am ſpeaking to. Their fear of coming to the ſacrament, leſt they ſhould come in an unprepared manner, ſufficiently diſcovers their temper of mind; indicating it to be religious, if not gracious. They would not offend God; they had rather omit duty, than do it under the apprehenſion they ſhould hereby diſpleaſe

please him. They are the subjects of a serious, if not a saving sense of God and divine things. It is their concern, that they might honour and serve him; and that they do not do it in the article under consideration is owing, rather to their reverence of the divine majesty, that the want of regard to his governing authority.

And are persons of this character essentially defective in their preparation for an attendance at the table of the Lord? It ought not to be supposed. It may rather be thought, they will be esteemed by our Saviour welcome guests. They had certainly better wait upon Christ at this ordinance, with this preparation, than totally absent themselves from it.

You say, you are afraid to come to the sacrament, lest you should come being unprepared for this sacred duty. Let me ask you hereupon, have you no fear upon your spirit, as taking rise from a total neglect of this gospel-appointment? Is there no sin, or danger, in a continued course of practically throwing disregard upon as express an institution of Jesus Christ, as any in the sacred books? There certainly is, my friends,

friends, both sin and danger in neglecting to remember the dying love of Christ in the way of his appointment; and both the sin and danger of this neglect, continued in from one period of life to another, are much greater, and ought therefore to be much more feared, than a meer defect in the degree of preparation. Let it be acknowledged, it is a fault to come to the sacrament, unless we are in some good measure prepared in the habitual frame of our minds; but it is a fault likewise, and a much greater one, totally to abstain from it. Our wisdom and duty therefore is, neither abstain from it, nor to come to it, but with a mind so far prepared for it, as that it may be our serious and upright desire and endeavour to honor our Savior, and reap advantage to our own souls. And let me add here, none are more likely to come in this prepared manner, than those who fear to come, lest they should be unprepared. This fear will influence them to a becoming care, that they may eat of this bread and drink of this cup, not in a thoughtless, customary manner, but in a religious frame of mind, as those who distinguish between the sacramental, and common bread and wine, looking upon them as the symbols

bols of Chriſt's body and blood, and partaking of them as ſuch, in the exerciſe of faith affection, zeal, and hearty deſires to be ſpiritually benefitted by them. It were to be wiſhed, all that come to this ordinance would come with this preparation of mind. It would, in this caſe, be better attended than it commonly is, more to the glory of God through Chriſt, and more to the edification of communicants in faith, and love, and comfort.

There are yet other difficulties to be mentioned. But theſe muſt be referred to ſome other opportunity. The good Lord bleſs what has been ſaid, that it may be beneficial to us.

A M E N.

SERMON

SERMON IV.

Acts. II. 42.

"*And they continued steadfastly—in breaking*
"*of Bread.*"

I Have taken occasion, from these words, to apply to several sorts of persons, in reference to their celebration of the sacramental-supper. The last I spake to were those, who would gladly remember their Savior and Lord in this way of his appointment, but that they are hindered by various perplexing doubts and fears. Some of these I have already mentioned, and endeavoured to remove.

The next difficulty, which I now proceed to consider, arises from a fear some have, lest they should not eat and drink at the supper of their Lord in that SPIRITUAL manner, without which they should only sin, if they should be guests at it. They imagine, they must be the subjects of SPIRITUAL life, or they cannot take of the bread, or wine; or eat of the one, or drink of the other, in the exercise of that faith and love, without which they should rather prophane the ordinance, than to attend on it to the honor of Christ, or the profit of their own souls. They had therefore, they conclude, better stay from it, until they are made spiritually "alive to God through Christ".

It is obvious to say in reply here, that no one can pray to God, read, or hear his word, or perform any religious duty in a spiritual manner, unless he is the subject of spiritual life. Fear therefore, as taking rise meerly from an apprehended want of this life, if consistent and uniform in its operation, will restrain persons from every instance of piety, as well as this of remembring their Saviour at the sacrament. They ought indeed, upon this principle, no more to pray, or hear God's word, or attend on any institution of religion, than this of the Supper.

For

For, not being possessed of spiritual life, they can no more perform the former of these duties in the spiritual sense, than the latter. And what are we now brought to in real consequence? Religion, in all its branches, must be neglected, by all who have not "passed from death to life". And does this comport, in any measure, with the requirements of the gospel? Was it the view of God, in instituting the means of religion, that that they should not be used, until one of the main ends, proposed by them is effectually answered without them? Was it his design, that persons should sit idle, and do nothing, until, by the power of his grace, they are changed into "new-men in Christ"? The holy Bible, that infallible rule of direction, no where suggests any thing to this purpose. On the contrary, it puts men upon the use of means as the way, and the only way, in which they may expect to be made "partakers of the divine nature". The "clean heart", and the "right-spirit", are, upon the gospel plan of mercy, obtainable blessings. But how are they to be obtained? Says the answer of God himself, "I will be inquired of to do this for you". And that is the advice of our Savior Jesus Christ, not to those

only

only who had grace already, but to those also who had it not, "ask, and ye shall receive; seek, and ye shall find; knock, and it shall be opened to you". And Simon Magus, though at present destitute of a principle of spiritual life, was yet directed by an inspired apostle "to pray God if perhaps he might be forgiven". Meerly the want of a spiritual principle cannot therefore be a good reason, why we should not be in the use of any instituted mean of religion. If it is, those ought not to pray, who are not spiritually alive to God. For they can no more spiritually perform this duty, than any other; and if duty may not be performed, unless spiritually performed, they may no more pray than "break bread" at the Lord's table. But persons, not spiritually alive, are not only allowed, but expresly directed, even by God himself, to pray to him: From whence it unquestionably appears, that meerly the want of spiritual life is not a valid reason, why duty, in any instance whatever, may not be attended.

There are, my brethren, other principles, besides that of spiritual life, from which persons may perform duty. They may do it from a principle of fear, "being persuaded

ded thereto by the terrors of the Lord"; they may do it from a principle of hope, expecting in this way to obtain the divine favour; they may do it from a principle of obedience, as having their minds impressed with a serious deep sense of the bonds of God that are upon them; yea, they may do it from a principle of faith that is real, though it should fall short of that which is saving: All which are good principles of action, though not the highest, and best.

AND, in consequence of these principles, that are good in themselves, they may perform duty also in a manner morally, if not spiritually, good; they may do it heartily, in opposition to hypocrisy; they may do it earnestly, in opposition to heedlesness and formality; they may do it with awakened affections, in opposition to dulness and coldness; yea, they may do it in the exercise of a real faith in God, and in his Son Jesus Christ, though their faith should not be that precious faith, which is peculiar to the justified through the redemption that is in Jesus Christ.

AND as duty in general, and as it respects the "breaking of bread" at the Lord's-table in particular, may be performed from

from such principles, and in such a manner, shall any live in the omission of it meerly, or only, because they cannot perform it from a principle, and in a manner, still higher and more noble? This, surely, is not right. It cannot be justified, either upon the foot of reason, or revelation.

It is readily acknowledged, when men, besides being destitute of a spiritual principle, have so little sense of the nature and obligations of religion, as that they can attend it's duties in a thoughtless, careless, customary manner; or engage in the performance of them, only that they may be in the fashion, or with a view to wear a cloak for reputation, or that they might the more advantageously carry on their worldly and carnal designs: I say, when, besides the meer want of spiritual life, persons are in a disposition thus to attend duty, they had as well not do it all. Perhaps, it would be less dishonorary to God, to omit it, than to perform it thus heedlessly and hypocritically. But shall the same be said of that performance of it before described? Shall those, who, though they are not spiritually alive, yet have upon their minds a serious sense of God and religion, and can attend it's duties with earnestness,

estness, affection, and faith; shall such as these discourage themselves herefrom, or be discouraged by others? It ought not to be. There is certainly a wide difference between thoughtless, senseless, secure sinners, and those who are earnestly concerned about the great affairs of religion, who are disposed to seek God with their heart, and to wait upon him in all the ways of his appointment, that they may be savingly enlightned, and quickned by him. The prayers of the former may be abomination to him, much more a participation of the symbols of Christ's body and blood; while he may regard the former, approving of their endeavours, in the use of the means he has appointed, in order to their being spiritually blessed by him. Did our Savior Jesus Christ ever discourage such from coming to him? Was he not rather moved with compassion towards them? Was he not particularly urgent with them to " to seek God that he might be found of them "? And were there none in the apostles days, not better qualified, who sat down at the sacramental supper? Those holy men of God gladly admitted multitudes of this sort to communion with them in " breaking of bread". And could they now speak from the excel-

lent

lent glory, I doubt not but they would say, their fears were groundless; they ought to get the better of them, and not suffer themselves, any longer, to be detained from so advantageous a mean of religion as that of the sacramental supper. And this leads me

To another difficulty in the way of some; and this is, an apprehension of the Lord's-Supper as intended, in it's appointment, for those only who are partakers of the grace of God in the special, or saving, sense. The ordinance, say they, is a privilege appropriated to persons of this character. No other have a right to it; and should they lay in a claim, it would be in the view of God nothing better than presumption. And as we are in doubt, whether our faith is that by which " the just shall do live", we doubt our having a right to the sacrament, and so had better stay from it, until we are well satisfied that we are believers unto life. This is a difficulty that has often layn heavy upon the minds of too many; either keeping them from the table of the Lord, or making their presence there uncomfortable, if not, at times, greatly distressing. To such I would say,

IF it is indeed the truth, that the sacramental supper is designed for those only who are endowed

dowed with saving grace, none but such ought to come to it: Nor ought any other to be encouraged to do so. This is a plain case, so plain as not to admit of dispute. And as their right to come, is, upon this supposition, essentially connected with their being the subjects of true grace, they must be well satisfied they have this grace, or they cannot, upon just and solid grounds, be satisfied that they have this right. Grace and right are, in the present case, so related to each other, that wherever there is the want of the one, there cannot be the other. And should any be in doubt, as to the truth of their grace, they must, in the same degree, be in doubt as to the validity of their claim to this ordinance. And to speak plainly, and without disguise, I must freely confess, I cannot see how any, who connect a right to the Lord's-Supper with the real truth of Grace, can, with a good conscience, come to it, unless they are clearly satisfied in their minds, that they are partakers of that unfeigned faith, which is proper only to the redeemed unto God by the blood of Christ. And was there no other reason to question, whether it is a truth, that the sacramental supper is appropriated to those only who are believers in

M   the

the saving sense, insomuch that none else may warrantably come to it, this I should esteem a very good one. For who then would eat and drink at the Lord's table, but those who had some good degree of assurance, respecting the safety of their spiritual state? And how few, alas, are these? It is truly a rare thing to meet with christians that have got above doubts and fears, relative to the goodness of their character in the gospel estimation. The table of the Lord must consequently, upon the impleaded supposition, be surprisingly thin of guests; unless those should appear at it, who had no right to be there, or, what amounts to the same thing, in the present case, who did not know that they had this right, or that were any other than bold intruders; for this they could no otherwise know, than by being beyond doubt as to the goodness of their state God-ward. Surely, it was never the intention of our Savior, in appointing, the sacramental supper, to limit an attendance at it to those few only, who had got above doubt or fear, as to their being christians in the saving sense; and yet, this must have been his intention, if those only may warrantably give their attendance, who are the subjects of true grace; because they must know
themselves

themselves to be so, or they cannot know they have any divine warrant to eat of this gospel-supper. The plain truth is, this restriction of a right to the sacrament, will at once exclude multitudes from it who are real christians, because they are weak and doubting ones. None such, if a right to this ordinance is connected with the reality of grace, ought to come to it. For, so far as they are in doubt of their being real good christians, they must doubt of the lawfulness of their being guests at it. And if they doubt of their right to be at the sacrament, they will incur the charge of guilt if they come to it. That saying of the apostle Paul, Rom. 14. 23, is as applicable in the case of doubting as to a right to the Lord's-Supper, as in the case he particularly mentions, "He that doubteth is damned * if he eat, because he

* The word, rendered here *damnation,* means the judgment of a man's conscience, fastening upon him the charge of guilt. And this it willdo, in the case the apostle is upon, if it does its proper office ; " because, (as he goes on to reason) he eateth not of faith," that is, he eateth, not being fully persuaded in his mind, that he might lawfully eat. And this is sin. For as it follows, in the

he eateth not of faith"; that is, he stands condemned in his own conscience, because he eats, not being fully persuaded it was lawful for him to eat. Thousands of those who the next words, "whatsoever is not of faith is sin"; that is, whatever a man doth, not being persuaded, so as to be beyond doubt, that he might lawfully do it, he sins in what he does. *Faith* stands here in opposition to *doubting*, and therefore means such a persuasion of mind as leaves no room for hesitation, as to the lawfulness of an action. The greek word translated here *doubteth*, is, as Mr. Lock observes, in Rom. 4. 20, translated *staggered*; and is there opposed to *strong in faith*; or to *fully persuaded*, as it follows in the next verse: And this exhibits the true meaning of the apostle, in the text we are upon. His words, it is true, were spoken with reference to eating, or not eating, meat that had been offered to idols. If a man doubted, whether he might eat of such meat, he would be now condemned, in conscience, if he did eat; because he did that which he was not fully persuaded in his own mind he might do. But his reasoning will hold equally strong in the case before us. If it is a man's professed principle, that he ought not to be a partaker of the sacramental supper, unless he is the subject of that faith which is connected with everlasting life, he will stand condemned by his conscience, if it judges rightly, as chargeable with guilt, if he partakes while *doubting*, whether he is possessed of this

who might be worthy communicants at the Lord's table, and receive great spiritual profit by being there, will be excluded from it, if those only may rightfully come to it, who can come, not doubting of the goodness of their character as christians. I cannot suppose our Lord has made the way to his table

this faith. If he is not so fully persuaded that he is, as to have got beyond doubt " he sins, because he does not this in faith "; that is, with a persuasion of mind, excluding all doubt, that he acts in this matter, as divinely warranted hereto. Whenever a man doubts of the lawfulness of an action, it is not possible he should do that action, believing that he may lawfully do it; that is, in the exercise of a faith that is opposite to, and excludes doubting, which means the same thing with a clear, full, and strong persuasion of mind; and unless he has this faith, or full persuasion of soul, he " sins", if we may believe the apostle Paul. Upon the principle therefore, that saving grace is a qualification, without which none have a right to partake of the Lord's-Supper, none ought to do so, until they are freed from all doubt as to their being thus qualified. Simple *hope* will not, in this case, be sufficient; no, nor a *prevailing hope*. A man must be so fully persuaded, as to have no doubt hanging about his mind. And should he have been a partaker of the ordinance of the supper an hundred times, if he found himself to be in a doubting state, with respect to the real truth of his character as one that
was

ble so strait and narrow; neither can I bring myself to think, that he ever intended this appointment of his religion to be an occasion of embarrasment to the minds of his disciples, those of them especially that are weak, or fearful, and need rather to be encouraged to, than deter'd from, the practice of their duty.

THE most proper and direct answer therefore to the difficulty under consideration is,

a was savingly converted, it would be his duty to observe this institution no more, until his doubt was removed: otherwise he would sin; for whosoever eats and drinks at the sacramental supper, according to the principle we are considering, not having a clearly full, and satisfactory persuasion in his own mind, that he is born of God, not only sins, but his conscience will tell him that he sins, if it is faithful to do its office.

In this view of the matter, which is an apostolic one, those who have not as yet been at the table of the Lord, ought not to appear there, neither should those dare to come again who have often been there, if in the state David was in, when he prayed, as in Psal. 51. "make me to hear joy and gladness—cast me not away from thy presence, and take not thine holy Spirit from me, restore unto me the joy of thy salvation, and uphold me by thy free spirit; or if in the state of those, Isai. 50. 10. who, though "fearers of the Lord, yet walked in darkness, and saw no light". In a word, if a right to the sacramental supper, and that

faith

a denial of the foundation on which it is built, namely, that saving grace is a qualification without which persons may not come to the table of the Lord. If those may warrantably come, as allowed by their Lord to come, who have not as yet attained to that faith faith by which a man is justified, are inseperably connected by the gospel constitution, no one, whether he never has been, or now is a communicant at it, ought to appear a guest there, unless he is sure that he is a believer to life, that is, so persuaded of this as to have no doubt about it in his mind. If these now are all excluded, and exclude themselves they must, or be condemned by their own consciences as chargeable with guilt if they do not: I say if all these are excluded, how amazingly thin will be the appearance of guests at the sacramental supper! By far the greater part in all our churches must no more come to this ordinance as communicants, until they are so satisfied of the goodness of their state, in the spiritual sense, as to be in no doubt about it: And, perhaps, there may be some churches to whom it ought not to be administred, there not being a sufficient number in them that can "eat in faith"; that is, with such a persuasion of their being the subjects of converting grace, as excludes all doubt from their minds. Perhaps, this may be the case with respect to some at least of their pastors; who then shall administer the ordinance to them? Surely, our Lord could never intend to make an attendance at his table a matter of almost constant perplexity to his disciples!

faith which is faving, all ground of perplexity from this quarter is at once removed away. And that this is the real truth, I shall endeavour to make evident to you. And that I may do it in the moſt eaſie, and yet moſt ſatisfying way, I ſhall turn your view to the practice of the inſpired apoſtles, in admitting perſons to communion with them in "breaking of bread"

AND was this ſuch as will countenance the thought, that nothing leſs than a faith that is ſaving will qualifie for the ſacrament, or that none who are not thus qualified, ought to come to it? Far from this, their practice obviouſly and unavoidably leads us to think juſt the reverſe; namely, that the ſacramental inſtitution was deſigned for the uſe and benefit of profeſſing believers in general, whether their faith is of the ſpecial, or common kind. It is certain, the ſeveral communities of chriſtians, in apoſtolic times, were conſtituted of two ſorts of believers; believers unto life, and believers whoſe faith was not an abiding principles of good action. And it is as certain that they all, unleſs excluded for open ſcandal, were partakers at the Lord's table, and this under apoſtolic direction; yea, as having ſome or other of the apoſtles at their head,

and

and leading in the administration. Nay, it is evident beyond dispute, that it was the practice of the apostles to admit professing believers to the supper of the Lord under circumstances, wherein neither they, nor the persons themselves, could, upon rational evidence, know, whether their faith was any other than that common one which would consist with their perishing beyond the grave. The three thousand persons we read of, in my context, as admitted to " break bread " with the apostles, were admitted to this gospel privilege, the very day they were convinced that Jesus was the Christ, and professed faith in him as such. And it is the truth of fact, that it was their practice to receive persons to communion with them, in all the privileges of God's visible kingdom, upon a bare profession of faith in Christ, without waiting for evidence from its fruits, that it was the faith by which " the just do live". We no where read, in the sacred books, of their delaying to baptise any, or to admit them to fellowship in the Lord's-Supper, until it was made evident either to them, or the persons themselves, that they were the subjects of that faith which is connected with salvation. Far from this, they

IMMEDIATELY

IMMEDIATELY baptised, and admitted to the sacrament, all that professed faith in the gospel-revelation; and upon this profession only. Surely, they would not have been thus hasty in their admissions to a participation in gospel ordinances, if they had thought, that christian professors might not, with the allowance of their Savior, join together in "eating and breaking bread", until they were the subjects of that faith which is justifying. Had this been their sentiment, it cannot be supposed, without dishonouring their character, that they would at once, without any delay, have owned all that made a profession of faith as disciples, admitting them to fellowship with themselves in all the privileges of the gospel dispensation. It might rather, with all propriety, have been expected, that they would have taken time to advise, caution, and guard their hearers; waiting for credible evidence, in the judgment of rational charity, that they were believers in the saving sense, before they allowed them to be partakers at the Lord's-Supper. Had they looked upon it as a truth, that this ordinance was intended by our Lord, in his appointment of it, for the use of those only who were believers unto life, it is unaccountably strange,

strange, that they should have encouraged, yea, directed such numbers to the use of it, upon a bare profession only, before there had been opportunity for the tryal of their faith, or the exhibition of reasonable proof that it was of the saving kind. They knew that our Lord had said to believers in him, " then are ye my disciples, if ye continue in my word". And again, " not every one that saith unto me, Lord, Lord, shall enter into the kingdom of heaven, but he that doth the will of my father which is in heaven". They knew also, from what they had seen themselves, that, among those who had professed faith in Christ, there were some, yea, a great many, whose faith did not " work by that love", either to God or man, which the gospel makes necessary to denominate it a faith that is saving. They could not therefore admit persons to christian fellowship in gospel ordinances, meerly, or only, upon a verbal profession of faith, looking upon this profession as credible evidence, that they were truly sanctified. For it was not in the judgment of the largest rational charity, good evidence in the case. Instead of being convinced, upon just and solid grounds, that it was a justifying faith, there was reason rather to fear, at least,

in

in regard of many, that it was no other faith than would leave them short of heavenly salvation. It ought not therefore to be supposed, when the apostles so suddenly admitted persons to baptism, and the Lord's-Supper, upon a bare profession of faith in Christ, that they imagined, that this profession gave credible proof that they were believers in the saving sense, or that they esteemed them as such. It is far more reasonable to think, on the contrary, that they understood, by the faith here professed, no more than such a conviction that "Jesus was the Christ", as to be therefrom disposed and influenced to a readiness to own him as their Savior and Lord; and, in consequence hereof, to put themselves under his care, guidance and tuition; and to be found in the use of his appointments, as the best method they could take to be further enlightened, improved, and trained up in the way they should go, in order to their finding eternal life. If gospel institutions are considered as a means wisely and powerfully fitted to cultivate and improve such a faith as this, and as designed by God for the use of those who have it, in order to their becoming christians, formed to a "meetness, for the inheritance of the sanctified by faith in Jesus Christ

Christ, the conduct of the apostles was exactly such as it was proper and reasonable it should be. It is beyond all doubt with me, that this was their sentiment concerning these institutions; and that this also was their view in admitting these professors to an attendance on them. Nor, unless they acted under the influence of this thought, and with this view, is it possible, as I imagine, to justifie either the wisdom of their conduct, or its faithfulness to God, or the souls of men: Nor can they be justified, upon any other scheme of tho't, who encourage persons in the use of gospel institutions, who are not clearly satisfied, upon proper tryal of their faith by its fruits, that it is of the saving kind.

The plain truth is, no good reason can be given, why the institutions of the visible kingdom of God should not be intended for the use and benefit of all professing christians, seriously concerned about their souls, and everlasting salvation; though their faith, at present, should be no other than that which is the effect of the ordinary illuminations and assistance of the divine Spirit. They are as suitably adapted to beget, as to increase, a faith that is saving. And it is, perhaps, in the serious, diligent, persevering use of these instituted

stituted means of grace, that persons, generally speaking, are made holy, really and truly so, as well as improved in this gracious quality of their minds. Men, it is true, must have faith in the gospel-revelation, before they can attend its institutions, unless they should do it from a principle of hypocrisy. Accordingly the apostles admitted none to christian communion, until they professed faith in Christ. * But, upon doing this, they received them into the kingdom

---

* It may be worthy of remark here, as those, to whom the gospel was preached in the apostles days, were either *Jews*, or *Gentiles*, they could have admission into the visible kingdom of Christ only by baptism, with a previous profession of faith in him as the Son of God, and Savior of the world. But then it ought to be considered, this profession they might make from a real and strong persuasion of mind that he was "the Son of God", and his religion that alone by which they could be saved; while, at the same time, their faith, which was the ground of their admission into Christ's visible kingdom, might fall short of that which would interest them in eternal life. Our Savior himself has put this beyond dispute, not only by declaring more than once, in express words, that "many who believed on him" were not believers unto life; but by a variety of parables, which he spake on purpose to convey this sentiment, that persons might be visible members of his kingdom, though

dom of grace; not waiting for evidence that they were already fit for the kingdom of glory, but putting them at once under the enjoyment of all gospel means, privileges, motives, and advantages, that they might,

though their faith was not of the saving kind; as you may read at large, in the 13th Chap. of Matthew's gospel. Nay, so far was he from supposing, that all that professed faith in him, and had thereupon been admitted, as disciples, into his visible kingdom, were the subjects of that " faith by which the just do live", that he not only compares many of them to *tares* growing up with the *wheat*; but solemnly prohibits their being " rooted up", and publishes it as his pleasure, that both be suffered to " grow together, until the time of the harvest". One reason of this, without all doubt, was, that they might, by the cultivation of gospel means, and advantages, be changed into *good wheat*. In the natural world this is impossible; but not so, in the spiritual kingdom of Christ. *Tares* may be, and often have been, converted into *wheat*: And one thing designed by our Savior in suffering tares to have a being in his church unquestionably was, that this conversion, under gospel culture, might be effected. In this respect, there is an *essential* difference between God's kingdom that is above, and his kingdom here on earth. None but such as have been partakers of the grace of God in truth shall have admission granted to them into the heavenly kingdom. And provision has accordingly been made to bring this into event. For one that infalibly knows " what is in

might, by a wise and good use of them, be made "men of God," formed to a "meetness for the inheritance of the saints in light." And it was doubtless, the design of God, in erecting

in man", is the appointed judge, with whom it belongs to determine, who the persons are that shall have entrance into heaven. And none but such as he knows, beyond the possibility of mistake, have been "sanctified through faith in him", shall see his face there. And had it been, in like manner, the intention of God, that none but the "renewed in the spirit of their minds", should be admitted into his visible church on earth, and partake of its visible privileges, he would, without all doubt, have taken sufficient care, so to have guarded the affair of admission as to have excludded all others. But this he has not done. There is no divinely constituted judge, or judges, on earth, either among the clergy or laity, considered singly, or as united in a body, who are qualified to make a *certain* judgment, respecting the real character of any of those who may desire to be admitted to fellowship in gospel ordinances; neither are the persons, who offer themselves, always able to make a just judgment of their own character, and never an absolutely certain one. Christ is the one only judge of the internal state of men; nor will this be *certainly* known, until the day of the revelation of his righteous judgment. It is, therefore, highly reasonable to think, that there is a difference between the terms of admission into the church on earth, and the church in heaven. If they were the same, it would be absurd erecting the gospel dispensation, with so many powerful, well adapted means and advantages, to train up all that are under it, as in a school, "from faith to faith," from a common faith to a special one, and from a special one in a lower degree, to an higher, until the subjects of it are complete in Christ.

ENOUGH has now been said to make it evident, to suppose, that no effectual provision should be made to keep those out of the church here, who are disqualified for an admission into the church of God that is above. The plain truth is, it is no where suggested, in any part of the old or new-testament, that all those who are members of the visible church here, and admitted to partake of its visible privileges, are really and certainly saints; or that, as such, they will hereafter be joined to " the general assembly, and church of the first-born, which are written in heaven". The intention of God, therefore, in erecting a visible kingdom, here on earth, with a variety of visible means, helps, privileges, and advantages, was not meerly, or only, to enlarge and brighten the qualifications of those, who are already *essentially* qualified for heaven; but to form those also to a meetness for it, who may as yet be destitute of this meetness: And the institutions of this kingdom are all of them so contrived, as to be, at once, equally and powerfully adapted, both to begin, and carry on, the work of sanctification in the souls of all that are members of it.

evident, that saving grace is not a qualification, without which persons may not come to the supper of the Lord.

Two things are commonly objected against what has been said, which it may be proper and needful to take some notice of here.

THE

I MAY properly subjoin here, the divinely appointed way, in which persons become members of the visible church of Christ, is utterly inconsistent with the supposition, that, in order to their being so, they must be the subjects of saving faith, or judged to be so. A profession of faith in Christ, in apostolic times, was *that*, without which, neither *Jews* nor *Gentiles*, of whom the world then consisted, could, by baptism, be admitted members of his visible kingdom. But how was it possible, that even the apostles, much less their successors in after ages, who could judge by the outward appearance only, not having it in their power to inspect the hearts of others, should be able to determine, whether the faith they professed was of the saving kind? And it is certain, it was not always of this kind, neither in the first times of the gospel, nor in any age since. Shall we say then, that those were not members in the visible kingdom of Christ, whose faith was short of that which is saving? This must be said, if saving faith is a necessary qualification in order to visible membership in the church of Christ. And will it not herefrom unavoidably follow, that it is impossible to know, who are, and who are not, members of Christ's visible kingdom? Yea, whether he has any such kingdom in the world? Be-

The first is, the case of the Ethiopian eunuch, who, upon desiring to be baptised, received that answer from Phillip, who had been expounding the scripture to him, "if thou believest with all thine heart, thou mayest." The plea here is, saving faith was, in

Besides, it ought to be remembered, that the children of those, who are members of Christ's visible church, are, by the constitution of God, from their first coming into existence, members of this kingdom in common with their parents. So it was under the *Jewish* dispensation. And so it is now under the christian; if there is any validity in one of the principal arguments, by which we vindicate our practice, in baptising the infants of those, who are members of Christ's church. We baptise them, because they are born disciples, members, in common with their parents, of the same visible kingdom, under the administration of Jesus Christ. Baptism is the badge, sign, or token of this privilege, by which they are distinguished from the children of those parents, who are without the pale of the church. With respect to *these*, who are by far the greater part of the visible kingdom of God, none will say, they were, when they first commenced members of this kingdom, the subjects of saving faith. A membership in the church of Christ was their birth-right, an absolute grant of the favor of God towards them. And members of this church they will be, whether their parents bring them to baptism, neglect to do so, or are hindered by the invented requirements of man. For baptism with respect to infants, is the mark of
Christ,

in regard of this person, made necessary in order to his being admitted to the ordinance of baptism. And if he might not be baptised without this faith, to be sure he might not be a partaker at the Lord's-table.

THE answer is easie. It is said, without sufficient reason, that " believing with all the heart"

Christ publicly owning them as members of his kingdom, not a rite by which they are admitted into it.

IT will, perhaps, be said here, should it be allowed, that the infant seed of believers are, in common with their parents, members of the kingdom of Christ, yet it must, at the same time, be affirmed, that this gives them no right, when they come to years, to special gospel ordinances. In order to this, they must profess saving faith in Christ, and explicitly covenant to be his : It is this, and this only, that instates them in this right. The reply is, if the gospel was to be preached to our native Indians, or to other pagan people, or to the Jews in any place whither they have been scattered, they would have no right, any more than those the apostles preached to, in their day, to special gospel ordinances, until, by a previous profession of faith in Christ, they had been admitted, by baptism, into that visible church of which he is head. But this cannot, with truth, be applied to those, who are already members of this church ; as is the case, with respect to such adults as had, in their infancy, the mark of disciples put upon them by the water of baptism. How far it may be expedient, as tending to edification, for *these* previously to their
coming

heart" means the same thing with saving faith. Many, in the days of Christ, and his apostles, heartily believed; yea, their whole heart was in their faith, insomuch that they received the word with joy, yea, a strong motion in all the passions and affections coming to special ordinances to profess faith in Christ, and openly covenant to be his, I dispute not at present. But thus much I will venture to say, that, their right to special ordinances is not at all founded on any such profession or covenant, but on their membership in the church of Christ. Being members of this church, as truly so as those who communicate at the table of the Lord, they have a divinely established right, when they come to years, to all the visible means, privileges, and advantages of the gospel visible kingdom: Nor has any church on earth a power delegated to them, from him who is head over all, to hinder them from the exercise of this right, unless their behavior is such as that, in a way of christian discipline, a stop is put to it conformably to the directions of the gospel. The plain truth is, they are either members of the visible kingdom of Christ, or they are not. There is no medium here. If they are members at all, they are as much so as they can be. It is not in the power of man to make them more, so then they are already. The owning the covenant, as it is called, that they may have baptism for their children, according to the manner of these churches; or their owning the same covenant, or a like one, that they may be admitted, as we commonly speak, to full communion,

fections of their heart; while yet, their faith was not as an abiding principle, as appeared afterwards, by their falling away in a time of temptation, or by their being led aside by the cares of the world. And this might have been the case of this eunuch, for ought any thing that is known to the contrary:

munion, makes no alteration as to their membership in the kingdom of the Son of God. They were before as truly, and as much members in this kingdom, as they are now. There are no *half members* in the visible kingdom of Christ. Whoever are members at all, are *whole* members; and, as such, have a right, at mature years, to a seat at the table of the Lord, unless, by their unchristian conduct, they have forfeited it. The churchs of Christ, I fear, are generally and greatly wanting in their duty to those, who are visible members of the same body with themselves, while they take little or no care, that they pay due honor to the special institutions of christianity. Instead of laying obstacles in their way, preventive of this, they should remove them so far as it is in their power; giving them all the encouragement, and assistance they may need. If they see their way clear to bring their children to baptism, and are seriously desirous of it, they should be permitted to do it; though religious fears and scruples should restrain them from coming to the table of the Lord; in which case, they should be instructed in meekness, with all long-suffering and forbearance. But, if their neglect of this ordinance should appear to arise from habitual carelessness

contrary: Besides, the eunuch, in answer to Phillip, did not say that he " believed with all his heart." His words import nothing more than single naked belief. Said he, " I believe that Jesus is the Son of God"; upon which he was straitway baptised. But if his answer had been, " I believe with all my heart, that Jesus is the Son of God", it would not have been evident, that he was the

lesness and inattention, discovering their contempt of it, they should be reproved and admonished; and, if finally obstinate in their contempt, they should, in the gospel way, be cut off from their relation to Christ,—But I may not carry this note to a greater length: Nor should I have so enlarged it, had it not been my view to signify my sentiments, with respect to some of the disputes of the present day; which appear to me founded on gross ignorance of the real nature of Christ's visible kingdom.

Since the penning the above note, and putting it into the printer's hands, I observed, upon occasionally looking over the records of the first church in Boston, of which I am pastor, the following questions, with an affirmative answer to them.

" Whether the relation of immediate children of church members be such, as giveth the church a church-power over them? And, consequently, whether it is the duty of the church to exercise that power regularly upon them, that their knowledge and life may be answerable to the engagements of their relation? And whether it be the church's mind, that solemn notice be

the subject of a faith that would have argued his being born of God : To be sure, he could not know that he was, upon just and solid grounds, unless by inspiration from above ; and without this, he would have been too hasty, and indeed rash, if his declaration concering his faith was intended to convey this thought.

It may possibly be thought by some, that "believing with all the heart" is too strong a mode of speech to mean any thing short of a faith that is connected with life. But it is a certain truth, that persons may believe in Jesus as the Son of God, and Savior of the world ; really in opposition to deceit, and hypocrisy ; heartily, in opposition to the want of affection ; and " with all their heart", as signifying the passionate emotion of their whole soul ; while yet their faith may have no depth

---

be given to them seasonably ? Voted by the church in the affirmative, on the 29th of the 11th month 1656. In agreement with this declared sense of the church, several acts of discipline are recorded ; particularly, the two following.

——" Son of our brother——of the age of 16 years, born and baptised into the fellowship of the covenant, for his choosing evil company, and frequenting a house of ill report, and that at unseasonable times, with

depth of root, and may leave them short of that renovation of mind without which they cannot be saved. It may be worth remembering here, it is said 2 Chron. 15. 12, that "all Judah entered into a covenant to seek the Lord God of their fathers with all their heart, and with all their soul". It follows in the 15th v. "and all Judah rejoiced at the oath; for they had sworn with all their heart: and God was found of them". Surely, no one will say, that, by "all the heart", in this passage, we are to understand a heart that had
P been

with bad persons, was called before the church, and admonished, the 3d of the 1st month, 1653".

—————" Being of the age of 21 years, born and baptised in the fellowship of this church, for his committing the sin of fornication, and his contempt of the church, that he would not come to hear them, was, in the name of the Lord Jesus, and with the consent of the church, excommunicated, on the 28th of the 4th month 1657.

I have here inserted the sense of this church, respecting their duty towards baptised persons, and their practice thereupon, in a way of discipline; because, as I imagine, they are truly scriptural, and if copied after, with due care and wisdom, would serve the church of God vastly more, than all that has ever been controversially wrote, about the right of persons that have been baptised to bring their children to baptism, or to "break bread" themselves at the table of the Lord.

been renewed by the grace of God. The most the phrase can be supposed to import is, that they entered into this covenant in real earnest, as having in motion the several passions and affections of their heart. So this eunuch believed, before he was baptised; and yet, neither he, nor they, might be the subjects of that sanctifying grace, without which they could not enter into that life which is eternal in heaven.

The other objection is taken from those words of the apostle Paul, which he spake with immediate reference to a participation at the Lord's-Supper, 1 Cor. 11. 28. "Let a man examine himself, and so let him eat of that bread, and drink of that cup". Now, a man's having, or not having, that faith which interests him in the purchases of the redeemer's cross, being an affair of the greatest importance, it is supposed, that this is the faith about which we are directed to examine our selves, and so go, or forbear to go, to the Lord's-Supper, as we find ourselves to be, or not to be, the subjects of it.

In answer whereto, I would say. It is readily acknowledged to be a matter of great importance to examine into our faith, that we may know, whether it is a faith that is connected

ed with falvation; and it may be fit and proper, as it would anfwer fome very good ends, thus to examine ourfelves, when we are about to go to the table of the Lord; though this is not the examination the apoftle has here in his view. The examination he directs to, does not fo much relate to the chriftian's character as favingly converted, as to his knowledge and faith, with reference to the facramental fupper. * The cafe was this, The Corinthians, to whom he was now writing, had been very

---

* The famous Henry Stephens, to whom our greek lexicographers are greatly indebted, and from whom they have greatly copied, affixes to *dokimazo*, as expreffive of its meaning, the words, *exploro, probo, experior, examino, æftimo*; and exhibits a number of examples, from the beft greek writers, of thefe feveral meanings of the word. And in all thefe fenfes, and perhaps in fome other, it is ufed in the new-teftament-books; examples of which might eafily be pointed out. But, inftead of this, I would rather obferve, that its *more fpecial* fenfe is always to be determined by its connexion in the difcourfe of which it is a part. It may alfo be worthy of remark, whether it fignifies, in any place, to *prove, approve, efteem*, or the like, the *bafis* of this meaning is, the true meaning of the englifh word, *examine*. I would further fay, to *examine, explore, fift* a matter by thorough inquiry, is moft frequently the fenfe in which *dokimazo* is ufed; though this fenfe is fignified

very irregular and disorderly in their celebration of the Lord's-Supper, for which the apostle, in this 11th chapter of his epistle to them, sharply reproves them; and, in order to rectify their disorders, he particularly relates in our bible-translation, by various english words of one and the same import. And this, as I judge, is its *proper*, or *more special*, sense in the text we are upon. When the apostle says, Dokimazetô de anthrôpos eauton", the translation in our bibles, "let a man examine himself", is, I imagine, as proper and just an one as could be given. For, let it be remembered, in order to rectify the disorders of the church at corinth, in relation to their observance of the sacramental supper, he had particularly recited to them the original institution, as he had received it from Christ himself: Upon which he immediately subjoins, "let a man examine himself, and so let him eat." To what end could he here set, before the view of the Corinthians, the pure, uncorrupt institution of the supper, if it was not, that, by examining their conduct by it, they might be influenced to behave better for the future. Surely, the duty here injoined them can be no other, than a trial of their " eating " the Lord's-Supper by the institution itself, in order to their comporting with the end proposed by it. His meaning may, I think, be clearly and fully expressed in the following paraphrase, let a man bring himself to the test of the institution, as I have given it in the words of Christ himself; let him examine, explore, try, and sift himself

;ates to them the institution of the supper, as he had received the account of it immediately from Christ himself, that, knowing its nature and design, they might observe it in a more worthy manner. In order whereto, his direction follows "let a man examine himself, and so let him eat of that bread, and drink of that cup". As if he had said, I have laid

self by it: In this way, he can be at no loss to determine, that his conduct will be greatly to blame, if he eats and drinks at the sacramental supper in that irreverent manner I have described, and am endeavouring to reform ; but will see himself obliged to do this in agreement with the nature, and design, of this sacred appointment : "And so let him eat" ; that is, conforming the manner of his eating to what upon examination, he finds it ought to be ; as what he does in this matter is, in obedience to a sacred appointment of Jesus Christ. And this same *trying, exploring, examining,* a man's self, by comparing his thoughts, his views, and his temper of mind, with the nature and design of the sacramental institution, as here recorded by the apostle, will, at all times, and with respect to all christians, in all places, have an happy and powerful tendency, not only to guard them against all irreverence and indecency in their celebration of the Lord's-Supper ; but to excite their care to eat of the bread, and drink of the wine there, so as that they may do this in a manner becoming so sacred a rite of the religion of Jesus Christ.

laid before you, in plain easie words, the nature and design of the sacramental supper, as instituted by Jesus Christ. Examine yourselves by this rule, and do it seriously, carefully and faithfully. This I advise you to, as a proper and suitable expedient to prevent your coming to this ordinance in the irreverent, indecent manner you have formerly done. In this way, you may come in a more worthy and becoming manner, to the honor of Christ, and your own spiritual profit. What the apostle aims at is, to put them upon duly distinguishing between this supper of the Lord, and their own, which they ate previous to it; looking upon it, not as a common meal, and partaking of it as such, but as an instituted memorial of Christ's dying love. This they might do, though their faith as yet was no other than that, which is the effect of the ordinary influence of the divine Spirit. Doubtless, a very considerable number of these Corinthians had no higher a faith than this; and if the apostle intended, that they should so examine themselves as not to come to the sacrament any more, unless they could find that they had saving faith, a very great part of this church must have abstained from the use of this ordinance. But this the apostle had not

in

in view. His only defign was, to direct to fuch an examination, more efpecially in relation to the facramental fupper, as might happily influence them to come to it in a more becoming manner, and as might reafonably be expected of thofe, who eat and drink of thofe fymbols, which figuratively reprefent the dying love of Chrift towards finners.

But the defign of the apoftle in this chapter will be more largely illuftrated, when I come to confider the next difficulty that hinders many ferious chriftians from an approach to the Lord's table. This is an important difficulty, and the occafion of perplexing fear to a great many. The confideration of it muft therefore be left to fome other opportunity.

I shall only fay further at prefent, It is not an eafie matter for chriftians, efpecially chriftians that are weak in faith, or that are but beginners in religion, to determine concerning their faith, that it is, not of the common, but faving kind. It would therefore be inconvenient and unfit to put them upon making this determination, previous to their going to the facrament, and as a qualification in order to it, and without which they might not attend at it. It would unavoidably throw the minds of many that are real christians, as well as other serious well-disposed persons, into perplexity and fear, and keep them from coming to this ordinance, though they might otherwise come to it with profit to themselves, and so as to honor their master Jesus Christ. I cannot suppose, the apostle would have given this occasion of distressing concern, as he must have done, in thousands of instances, if the examination he directs to, in this text, refers to a determination of our faith as saving, in order to our going to the sacrament.

THE good Lord bless what has been now said to the removal of those fears, which keep any from the table of the Lord; and may there, for the time to come, be seen a greater number of welcome guests at it!

A M E N.

SERMON V.

Acts. II. 42.

And they continued steadfastly—in breaking "of Bread"

I HAVE taken occasion from this text, to speak to those whose minds are perplext with difficulties, which keep them from attending the sacramental "breaking of bread." Several of these difficulties have been already mentioned, and that said which was thought sufficient for the removal of them.

I now proceed to another difficulty, and that which, perhaps, has been the greatest obstacle in the way of many serious well-disposed christians to the Lord's-table; and this is, a fear of "eating and drinking unworthily", and hereupon becoming "guilty of the body and blood of the Lord", and sealing "damnation to themselves". This fear has unhappily taken rise from a mistaken apprehension of those words of the apostle Paul, 1. Cor. 11. 27, "whosoever shall eat this bread, and drink this cup of the Lord unworthily, shall be guilty of the body and blood of the Lord". And again, ver. 29, "He that eateth and drinketh unworthily, eateth and drinketh damnation to himself, not discerning the Lord's body."

The readiest, and most effectual way, as I imagine, to obviate this difficulty, and give ease to the minds of those who may be perplexed with it, will be to be particular and distinct in ascertaining the precise meaning of the apostle, in the phrases he uses in these texts, "eating and drinking unworthily"; being "guilty of the body and blood of the Lord"; and "eating and drinking damnation to himself"; and then in applying what may be offered to the

the case of those, who may be under perplexing fear, from these passages of sacred writ, in a few remarks, or observations, suited to give them relief and help.

I shall, in the first place, endeavour, with all plainness, to open the meaning of the apostle in the above recited words, that have been the occasion of difficulty to serious christians.

Only, before I come to this, I would make a previous note, and desire it may be particularly attended to, and all along remembered, in the following discourse. It is this. The passages we are going to explain are not independant sentences, the proper meaning of which is to be gathered, from the meer force of the words, in themselves simply, and nakedly considered, but parts of a well cohering discourse; and can therefore be explained in no way, but by considering the design in view, the part they bear in the discourse, and how they stand connected with it. The not duly considering these things is, I believe, the reason their true meaning has so often been unhappily misunderstood. "Eating and drinking unworthily" at the Lord's table, considered in general, will never lead one into the true meaning of it in this place; because the apostle
is

is speaking of a special case, and the particular unworthiness of a particular number of christians, which can be known in no way, but by consulting the context. The nature and meaning of this "unworthiness" and the "special punishment" incurred by it, must be measured by that, and by that alone; unless it may be thought allowable to break in upon the apostle's course of reasoning, and put a sense on his words that has no pertinency to the design he is upon; which is certainly an unfair treatment of an human writing, and ought much less to be practised in regard of one that is sacred, as being of divine inspiration.

Having made this remark, the way is clear to look into the context, as the only proper method to understand the apostle, in the phrases we are about to explain. And by doing this we shall find, that great disorders, particularly with reference to the sacramental supper, had crept into the Corinthian church. It was on account of these disorders, that the apostle wrote this chapter; and if we would know, what that "unworthy eating and drinking" is, which he blames these Corinthians for, and would rectify for time to come, we must know what the indecences, and disorders were, that prevailed among them. For this
un-

"unworthiness" muſt be explained by theſe diſorders.

The apoſtle, before he comes to particular inſtances of their miſconduct, declares in general, as in the 17. ver. " I praiſe you not, that you come together not for the better, but for the worſe". More is intended in theſe words than is expreſſed. Their meaning is, far from commending you, I think you are greatly to be blamed. What I rebuke you for, and with ſeverity too, is, that, when you aſſemble together for the performance of the public offices of religion, you behave ſo as that your coming together, inſtead of being for your ſpiritual advantage, tends rather to the increaſe of your guilt.

Having ſpoken thus generally, he now comes to particulars; mentioning the ſpecial inſtances, wherein they were blame worthy. And they are theſe that follow.

The firſt is, their having diviſions among them. Says he, (ver. 18.) " when ye come together in the church, I hear there are diviſions among you; and I partly believe it." It ſhould ſeem it was by report from others, and not perſonal knowledge, that he became acquainted with this diſorder in the church at

at Corinth. But such was his intelligence, that he believ'd it "in part", or rather, fully "of part" of the church. And a scandalous disorder this was. The word, (in the original *Schismata*) here translated *divisions*; means, not meerly, or only, divisions in their *affections* towards each other, but divisions in their *outward conduct*. It is true, they met together in the same place for communion at the Lord's-Supper, but it was in a schismatical manner, dividing themselves into parties, and not appearing, as they ought to have done, as *one body*, affectionately united in commemorating the dying love of their common Lord. It cannot be deduced from any thing that is said in this chapter, or in any part of the epistle, that they had as yet separated from each other under the form of different *sects*, meeting in different places for worship: but the apostle tells them, that so it might be expected it would be. The prejudices, the lusts, and unsubdued tempers of men would lead to this, and God in his righteous providence might permit it, that it might be made to appear who, upon trial, would be approved as stedfast and immoveable. So his words run, ver. 19, " For there must be also heresies [in the original,
Airefeis

Aireseis, sects *] among you, that they which are approved may be made manifest among you". But though this corinthian church was not at present divided into two, or more separate societies, but continued one christian community, meeting together in the same place, yet they behaved in their assemblies in an unbrotherly, factious and schismatical manner. The apostle, accordingly, applies to them, as in the 20 ver. " when ye come together therefore into one place, † this is not to

---

* THE english word, *heresie*, is, by ecclesiastical writers, most commonly, if not always, restrained in its meaning to *doctrinal tenets*, supposed to be dangerously corrupt ; but this is not the sense of the greek word, *airesis* from whence it is derived, as used in the new-testament-books. It rather means what we call a *sect*, or people in a state of seperation from others, and meeting together as a different denomination. I have looked over all the places in the new testament, where the word is used, and find that this is the sense in which it is to be understood, in every text, one only excepted, which may admit of dispute.

† THE phrase, in the original, epi to auto, being of the neutral kind, may as well signifie *with the same design, for the same thing*, as *to one place* ; and it is accordingly often so to be understood. But the translation here, *to one place*, best suits the connection, as I imagine.

to eat the Lord's-Supper." As if he had said, though you assemble, as a christian society, in one and the same place, and there eat; yet you do it after such a manner, that it would be a dishonour to a sacred institution of Christ, to speak of it as eating the Lord's-Supper. This leads to

A NUMBER of other faults, these Corinthians are obviously charged with, and severely reproved for; as we may see, in the 21, and 22d ver. in which they are thus addressed, "in eating every one taketh before other his own supper, and one is hungry, and another is drunken. What! have ye not houses to eat, and to drink in? or despise ye the church of God, and shame them that have not? shall I praise you in this? I praise you not"?

THEIR having a "supper of their own" in the house of God, when about to celebrate the supper of the Lord, is here evidently spoken of as indecent and irregular. When the apostle says, "every one eateth before other his own supper", it is easie to perceive, that he alludes to a custom which had obtained among them, whatever gave rise to it, namely, that of having a common feast in the place of worship, here called "their
own

own supper," * either previous to, or mixed with, the " Lord's-Supper." This he plainly condemns, and would represent as a disorder unhappily introduced among them. What else can be the meaning of those severely reprehensive interrogatives, " what, have ye not houses to eat and to drink in ? or despise ye the church of God" ? As if he had said, Is it

not

---

* THERE is no room to question, whether christians, in the apostolic age, and afterwards, had their *feasts*, their *agapæ*, that is, their *love* or *charity feasts*. Jude speaks of these feasts ; so does Ignatius, which may give some a favorable opinion of them ; so do Clement of Alexandria, Tertullian, and others. It does not appear, from any thing that is said in any passage in the new-testament books, that these feasts were a divinely instituted preface, or appendix, to the Lord's-Supper. They were, without all doubt, the invention of man. Probably, they might take rise, with respect to both *Jewish* and *Gentile* converts to the christian faith, from the same general cause.

WE all know it was *after* our Lord had eat the *passover-feast* with his disciples, that he eat with them *his own supper* ; and he did it with what remained of the passover bread and wine, first solemnly separating them to the special use of remembering him. The *Judaizing christians*, under the guidance (it is likely) of *Judaizing teachers*, introduced of their own heads, tinged with jewish superstition, a supper previous to the Lord's, as the Lord's-Supper, when first instituted, was preceeded with the passover-supper.

And

not to your difgrace, and can you do any other than think fo, that you make the houfe of God a place for common feafting, when you have houfes of your own, you may ufe to this purpofe, as proper occafions may be offered therefor ? Your confciences, duly enlightened, will reproach you for fuch unfuitable conduct. I cannot but fuppofe, that thefe fuppers, in the place of worfhip, and conjoined, as it were, with the Lord's, let them be called *love-feafts*, or by whatever other name

And this previous fupper of their's might, as to the principles of its introduction, favor fo much of that which was *Jewifh* in religion, as to give occafion of offence to the *Gentile* chriftians.

On the other hand, the *Gentile* chriftians, as the Lord's-fupper was confequent upon a feaft, fome of the meterials of which were fet apart and confecrated in remembrance of Chrift, might think it proper to preface the fupper of the Lord with one of their own, making ufe of the bread, and wine of their own fupper in their obfervance of our Lord's. And there may be the more reafon to give this rife to this previous fupper among the greeks, as it is known to have been their cuftom to have focial feafts or fuppers. I would add here, this *previous fupper*, thus differenced as to the cirumftances attending its rife, with refpect to the *Jewifh* and *Gentile* chriftians, might be one occafion of the *(Schifmata) divifions* there were among them, and complained of by the apoftle in the 18th ver.

name, are here folemnly prohibited by the apoftle; efpecially, when he adds, "fhall I praife you in this? I praife you not." He could fcarce, in any way of diction that was more ftriking, have expreffed his condemnation of this practice among them.

ANOTHER irregularity they are rebuked for, is, their confounding, or fo mingling, "their own" with the "Lord's-Supper," that they were neither properly, nor fufficiently diftinguifhed from each other, as they ought to have been. It is with fpecial reference to this diforder, that the apoftle charges them, ver. 29, with "not difcerning the Lord's body", or, as the original words, [*mê diakrinôn*] might, perhaps, be more properly rendered, "not differencing *, not difcriminating, the Lord's body," that is, the facramental bread, figuratively called by our Savior in the inftitution of "his fupper,", and by the apoftle Paul in this chapter, "the body of Chrift", from

---

* So the original word means, and is tranflated to mean, in the following texts, Act. 15. 9. 1. Cor. 4. 7. Jude ver. 22. And this, undoubtedly, is its more fpecial meaning here; leading us to think, efpecially comparing this 29th with the 33d ver. that one thing the Corinthians are blamed for is, their eating the Lord's-Supper as a part of their own, or fo mingling them together, as not to preferve a due diftinction between them; which moft certainly they ought to have done.

from the bread of "their own supper." And in their way of celebrating the "supper of the Lord", it is plain it was not suitably differenced, or discriminated, from their "own supper"; nor did it appear, as it ought to have done, an open, solemn, religious declaration, or shewing forth, of his death.

ANOTHER fault still they are charged with is, their so eating their own supper as to betray a want of that kindness, yea, that common decency, which would have been blameworthy in those who knew nothing of christianity. By comparing the 21st with the 33d ver. we shall find, that they did not "tarry for one another", but as they came to the place of worship fell to, as the vulgar phrase is, and eat every one of what he had brought; by which means those who had brought a plenty were satiated, while those who, being poor, had brought nothing, were made ashamed, not having wherewithal to keep them from hunger. A strange manner of conduct this! It not only discovered the present inoperation of that brotherly kindness, which is the glory of a christian, but downright incivility; and they are both aggravated, as they were now purposely assembled, and assembling,

that

that they might unite in celebrating a sacred rite of the religion of Jesus. *

The last, but greatest disorder, among these

---

* The disorder complained of, in the above paragraph, always appeared unaccountable to me, until I had the opportunity of reading Raphelius's "philological annotations"; where I met with these words, vol. ii. pag. 344, "moris fuit athenis"—that is, " it was a custom among the athenians, in the age of Socrates, for persons who came to a supper, to bring every one of them something for himself; which was not made common to all, but for the most part every one eat that which was his own. An example of this he holds out to view from Xenophon, in his "memorab". lib. III. pag. 623 ; which is as full an illustration of this disorder among the Corinthians as can be desired. The words are these ; " *Opote de*"—In english thus, " when of those who came together that they might sup, some had brought with them a very little, others a great deal of provision, Socrates ordered a lad to put the little in common, or to distribute to each a part: In consequence of which, those who had brought a plenty with them were both ashamed not to partake of what was served up in common, and not to produce their own. They therefore put down their provisions in common, and because they enjoyed no more than those who had brought but little, they desisted from expending much in procuring victuals". It should seem, from this citation, that even a Socrates was ashamed of that disorderly conduct among the pagan Greeks, at their *collation suppers*, which appears to have been continued among the Corinthians after their conversion to christianity.

these Corinthians, was their *excess,* or *intemperance*; which, at any time, is highly criminal, but eminently so when about to eat bread, and drink wine, at the sacramental supper. The charge against them, in the 21st ver. is, not only that, "in eating every one taketh before other his own supper", but that, while "one is hungry, another drunken". It has been thought scarce possible, that these christians, especially while together in order to celebrate so solemn a rite as that of the Lord's-Supper, should be chargeable with *drunkenness,* literally and grosly speaking. Expositors therefore have commonly understood the word here in a more lax sense; supposing the most that can be meant by it is, that they had used too great freedom at their "own supper", eating and drinking to a degree of excess; and that, in this unsuitable frame, they partook, some of them, of the sacramental bread and wine. And this was the thought I was led to entertain of this matter, until I had given it a more critical examination; since which I imagine, it may justly be suspected, that some, among those who had brought a sufficiency for a full repast, were guilty of intemperance in too gross a sense of the word. *

* The principal reason inclining me to judge, that some of the christian professors at Corinth, were chargeable

THESE now were the indecencies and irregularities of the Corinthian chriſtians, with reference to the holy ſacramental ſupper. Accordingly, that *ſpecial unworthineſs,* I am explaining, which the apoſtle would faſten upon them,

chargeable with intemperance in a worſe ſenſe than expoſitors commonly ſuppoſe, is this. The word, *Methuei,* here tranſlated, *is drunk,* really means, in all its grammatical variations, throughout the new-teſtament, and is accordingly tranſlated in our bibles ſo as to mean, this kind of intemperance, one place only excepted ; which, perhaps, had as well been tranſlated, ſo as to carry a ſenſe more nearly agreeing with that, in which all the others are taken, as we may ſee preſently. In the mean time I would obſerve, the ſubſtantives, *Methué,* and *Methuſos,* are to be met with in five texts : the former in three, Luk. 21. 34. Rom. 13. 13. Gal. 5. 21. ; the latter in two, 1 Cor. 5. 11, and 6. 10. The verb paſſive, *Methuſkomai,* is found in three places, Luk. 12. 45. Eph. 5. 18. 1 Theſ. 5. 7. The verb active, *Metheuō,* is uſed, beſides in John 2. 10, the excepted place, in Matt. 24. 49. Acts 2. 15, in the text we are upon, in Theſ. 5. 2. Rev. 17. 2, and in the ſixth verſe : In all which texts, it not only ſignifies, but by our tranſlators is made to ſignifie, a groſsly faulty exceſs in drinking. It would therefore carry with it the appearance of a deſign to ſerve a cauſe, ſhould we depart, in this place, from the invariably tranſlated, as well as genuine ſenſe of the word, wherever it is to be met with in the new-teſtament books : Nor is it eaſily ſuppoſeable,

them, muft be confidered in connection here-with, and interpreted hereby. It accordingly means, in one word, the fame thing precifely with their celebration of the Lord's-Supper in that diforderly, irreverent, and prophane manner that had been mentioned. The

able, the apoftle would have ufed this word, which has fo bad a meaning, if he had intended only fome light degree of excefs. It will, probably be faid here, it would be too great a reflection on any of thefe chriftians to fuggeft, that they were intemperate to the excefs that has been mentioned; and that the want of candor only could influence any to put fo fevere a fenfe on the word ufed by the apoftle. The plain anfwer is, the apoftle would not have ufed this word, if he had not intended to convey by it the fenfe it is always taken in, and by himfelf too, every where in the facred books. The charge therefore of too great feverity in reflecting upon thefe chriftians, if juft, muft light upon the apoftle, and not on thofe who interpret his words according to their invariable ufe, both in the gofpels, and epiftles. The only way to exprefs candor towards them is to obferve, in mitigation of their fault, which was a very grofs one, that intemperance at *collation fuppers*, among the *Greeks*, had been common; and the *paſſover meal*, among the *Jews*, was allowed to be a full one; and too often it was carried into excefs. If therefore fome of thefe chriftians, whether from judaifm, or gentilifm, through the force of habit not fully eradicated, and by being off their guard, had been unhappily betrayed into what may be juftly called in-

temperance

The apostle is to be understood, as if he had said, he that eateth and drinketh in the manner I have pointed out, is the *He* that "eateth and drinketh unworthily". These things are connected in his discourse, and explain each other.

But some, perhaps, will say, is this all the *unworthy* eating and drinking at the Lord's table, that guests there may be chargeable with? I answer at once, without the least hesitation, no, by no means. There are other ways, wherein persons may bring upon themselves

temperance in drinking, it ought not to be looked upon as incredible. Dr. Whitby's note on the word, *Oi de metheuei*, and another *is drunken*, I shall think proper to insert here. Says he, "This may either refer to the *Gentile* converts among the corinthians, retaining still their *heathen* custom of drinking liberally after their sacrifices, whence *methuein, to be drunk*, is, by grammarians, thought to have its original from *meta to thuein*, because of the free drinking they indulged to after their sacrifices; or to the *judaizing* converts, who thought themselves obliged to drink plentifully at their festivals, four large cups of wine, says Dr. Lightfoot, at the *Paschal-supper*, and to be quite drunk, says Buxtorf, in the feast of *Purim*".—I have now given my opinion. Let every one judge for himself.

It was said just now, there was a text, John 2. 10, in which the same word, that is here used by the apostle, is translated in our bibles, well drank"; not importing any criminal degree in drinking. There was

no

felves this guilt. All such do so, who eat and drink of the sacramental bread and wine in a careless, thoughtless, inattentive, customary manner; much more may unworthiness be charged upon those, who come to the supper of the Lord to serve their reputation, or that they may be under better advantage to carry on their worldly designs; and it may in a worse sense still, and in as bad an one as

no need of giving the word so low a sense, and so different an one from that in which it is every where else taken in the new-testament. For, let it be observed, what is here said was spoken, not by our Savior, nor as insinuating a charge against any of the present guests, but referring to what had been a custom upon such occasions. The word, *methusthôsi*, might therefore here have well enough been translated in a sense nearer to the genuine import of the word, in other texts of the new testament. The "new version of the new-testament", by an anonymous author, has it thus, "when the guests had drank pretty freely". Harwood, in his late "translation of the new-testament", gives it this sense, "when the taste of company was blunted with drinking". And if it had been literally and strictly translated, "when they were overcome with drink", it would, as I imagine, have been but a fair and just version; nor would such a one have carried with it the least reflection, either upon our Savior, or any of the guests with whom he was now at a wedding. The word refers wholly to a custom, in that day at wedding-feasts; when if some of the company had drank too much, it would not have been strange; and, perhaps this was no uncommon thing.

as can eaſily be conceived of, be faſtened on your irreligious, prophane men, who, without any becoming ſenſe of God, or regard to his Son, but ſolely with a view to qualify themſelves for ſome poſt of honor, or profit, kneel before the altar, and take into their polluted mouths the ſacred ſymbols of the body and blood of Chriſt. In a word, it may juſtly be ſaid of all, that they eat and drink unworthily, who do not do it conformably to the nature and deſign of this inſtituted rite, and as it is fit and reaſonable it ſhould be done. But all this notwithſtanding, the *ſpecial unworthineſs,* the apoſtle is here ſpeaking of, is that ſchiſmatical, diſorderly, non-differencing, and intemperate attendance at the ſacramental ſupper, which he had been blaming, and condemning, the Corinthians for: Nor can any be guilty of "unworthily eating and drinking" in that ſpecial ſenſe, in which this fault is charged upon this chriſtian ſociety, unleſs they eat and drink at the holy ſupper of the Lord, in the like indecent, irregular, and prophane manner which they did.

HAVING thus explained the firſt words, that have been the occaſion of difficulty to ſerious minds, "He that eateth and drinketh unworthily", I go on to do the ſame by the next, "ſhall be guilty of the body and blood

blood of the Lord". Some, through weakness, the undue influence of fear, or a mind unhappily tinctured with superstition, have been kept from the sacramental supper, being led, by these words, to imagine, that, should they unworthily partake of it, they would be chargeable with the very sin the Jews were, when, literally speaking, they "wounded the body, and shed the blood of Christ". But this is so vain an imagination, so gross a contradiction not only to the known use of these words in scripture, but to common sense, that the bare mentioning of it is sufficient to expose it as ridiculously absurd. "The body and blood of Christ", here spoken of, are to be interpreted, not in the literal, but figurative sense. They mean, not "his real body and blood", but these symbolically considered, or as represented under the emblematical signs of "bread and wine", at the sacrament. So the words were meant by our Savior in the institution of the supper, and so they are understood by the apostle Paul in this very chapter, in the account he has given of the original consecration of "the bread and wine".

ACCORDINGLY, when it is said of those, who "eat and drink unworthily" at the sacrament,

ment, that they are "guilty of the body and blood of the Lord", the true meaning is, that they juſtly expoſe themſelves to that judgment God will inflict upon thoſe, who make an undue, ſinful, and prophane uſe of that "bread and wine", which, ſacramentally, figuratively, or ſymbolically, are "the body and blood of Chriſt". What this judgment in ſpecial is, as threatned in this chapter, we go on to ſhow, under the laſt words we propoſed to explain, namely,

"Eating and drinking, damnation to one's ſelf", in caſe of eating and drinking "unworthily" at the Lord's table. The engliſh word, *damnation*, does not anſwer to the true import of the greek word (*Krima*) here uſed by the apoſtle. And it is a thouſand pities it was thus tranſlated, as it has been, unhappily, the occaſion of much perplexity to many ſerious good chriſtians. Says the excellent Dr. Doddridge, in his note upon this word, "I think it the moſt unhappy miſtake in all our verſion of the bible, that the word, *Krima*, is here rendered *damnation*. It has raiſed a dread in tender minds, which has greatly obſtructed the comfort, and edification, they might have received from this ordinance". I fully join with this great and good man in the ſentiment here expreſſed ; and the rather, becauſe, having

ving confulted all the expofitors, and writers upon the facramental fupper, I could come to the fight of, I find, that they unite as one in fpeaking of the "judgment", more especially intended here by the apoftle, as of the temporal kind, not of "damnation" in the future world. It is true, this word (*Krima*) is fometimes ufed to fignify the damnation of hell; but it oftner means judgment in this prefent ftate. The apoftle Peter fays, (1. Epif. 4. 17.) "The time is come, when judgment (*Krima*) is to begin at the houfe of God". Will any one fay, damnation to future wrath is the judgment here meant? It cannot be fuppofed. The evangelift Luke (chap. 23. 40.) brings in one of the malefactors, who were crucified with our Lord, rebuking the other in thefe words, "doft thou not fear God, feeing thou art *(en to Krima)* in the fame condemnation"; that is, adjudged to one and the fame temporal death: Yea, in the 24th chap. 20th ver. he fpeaks of the chief priefts, and rulers, as having delivered our Lord *(en Krima thanatou)* to be condemned to death: Not furely to damnation in a future world. It would be blafphemous to fuggeft fuch an untruth. From thefe texts it appears, that the word (*Krima*) we are now explaining, may, agreeably to its ufe elfewhere in fcripture,

mean,

mean, not punishment in hell, but temporal evil in this world.

AND that this was the judgment the apostle had directly in his eye, when he made use of the word *Krima*, which, in our bibles, is translated "damnation", he has taken all proper care to put beyond all reasonable dispute. For, let it be particularly minded, in the verse immediately following that wherein he says, "he that eateth and drinketh unworthily, eateth and drinketh damnation to himself", he adds, as though on purpose to prevent our mistaking his meaning, in the use of the word translated damnation, " FOR THIS CAUSE, many are weak, and sickly among you, and many sleep". As if he had said, your disorderly, prophane manner, at the sacramental supper, has brought down upon you the judgments of God. *For this cause*, on account of this your unworthiness, he has visited you [perhaps, a miraculous visitation may be here intended] with bodily diseases, and temporal death itself: And this you have had exemplified among you, in many instances of those, who have been sick, and died. But to make it yet more certain, that by this *Krima*, which has been unhappily translated by the english word "damnation", in our bibles, we are to understand temporal judgment, and not the miseries of hell, the

apostle,

apostle, in the 32d ver. has expresly assigned, the reason of the infliction of the punishment (*Krima*) he had spoken of. His words are these, "when we are judged, we are chastened of the Lord, that we might not be condemned with the world". You observe, the evil, or punishment, be it what it may, to which these Corinthians had been adjudged, for their unworthy behaviour at the Lord's table, is here considered, by the apostle himself, as *disciplinary* only, a "divine chastening"; and as inflicted too, with a view to *prevent their damnation* in the other world. It is impossible therefore, the punishment, he here connects with this unworthiness, should mean, being of the medicinal kind only, any other than temporal judgment. In a word, the apostle, far from giving the least countenance to the sense of the word *Krima*, as translated "damnation", and meaning the "damnation of hell", has said that which is obviously and abundantly sufficient to lead every intelligent reader to understand by it, *temporal punishment*; such as had been inflicted upon some of these Corinthians, but in a way of *discipline* only, and in order to prevent their *damnation*, beyond the grave, with the wicked world.

IT will, perhaps, be asked here, does not unworthy eating and drinking at the Lord's
table

table expose to damnation in the other world? I answer; without all doubt it does. And so does unworthy hearing of God's word, unworthy praying to our father who is in Heaven, and unworthy performing any duty whatever in religion. The exact truth is, every sin, of whatever kind, or in whatever degree, whether it be a sin of omission, or commission, does as really expose to damnation, as unworthy eating and drinking at the Lord's-Supper.

But this notwithstanding, *future damnation* is not the punishment, the apostle more immediately intends, in the passage we are upon; but, as has been said, temporal *evil*, which he explains by these words, "weakness, sickness, and the sleep of death": Neither does he connect, even, this temporal judgment with every sort, or degree, of unworthy receiving the sacrament; but with that grosly irreverent, and prophane manner, in which the Corinthians received it. So that none have any just reason to apply that special punishment, here spoken of, be it what it may, to themselves, unless they can charge themselves with attending on the ordinance of the supper in the like wicked manner, which these Corinthians did; which is not much to be feared at this day. Their scandalous irregularities

larities, especially their divisive, intemperate manner at the Lord's-Supper, for which God, perhaps beyond the ordinary course of nature, sent sickness and death among them, are not the faults we are in present danger of falling into the commission of. Those, to be sure, are at the utmost distance from this unworthiness, who come not to the sacramental table from a consciencious fear, lest they should be chargeable with it. They, of all persons in the world, have the least reason to apply this text to themselves. Their case as widely differs from that of these Corinthians, as light differs from darkness. And as their cases are thus altogether different, it is quite beside the apostle's intention, and a downright abuse of his words, to perplex their minds, and discourage themselves from duty, in consideration of that, which is no ways applicable to them.

I MAY not improperly subjoin a few words here, in order to undeceive those, who ground a fear, from this passage of the apostle we have been upon, lest they should be certainly and unavoidably *damned,* should they happen to eat and drink at the sacramental supper, in an unworthy manner. This, I have reason to think, has given perplexing uneasiness to some serious souls, restraining them from remembering

remembering Chrift in the way of his appointment. But they have herein grofsly impofed upon themfelves. Should it be fuppofed, that the apoftle was fpeaking, in this text, of damnation in the coming world, which we have feen abundant reafon to think he is not, he ought by no means to be underftood, as meaning, that it would inevitably prove damnation to a perfon, fhould he come to the table of the Lord, and eat and drink there in an unworthy manner. For the gofpel of the blefled God has provided, through Chrift, and promifed, pardoning mercy to repenting finners, however many, or heinous, their fins may have been. Unworthily receiving the facrament may therefore, in common with all other unworthinefs, be forgiven by the intervention of repentance, and fo damnation be prevented. Should a perfon unhappily come to the fupper of the Lord, fo as to be an unworthy gueft there, through negligence, carelefsnefs, or any other faulty caufe, he might, by the grace of God, be brought to repentance; and this would as certainly fecure him from damnation, as it is true, that God is " ready to pardon", and embrace penitent finners in the arms of his mercy. Without all doubt, many are now in heaven, and many will, in time to come, have admiffion into this blefled place, who

have

have often been at the sacramental table in an unworthy manner: not because it was not their sin; but because, by repentance, they obtained the forgiving mercy of God.

I HAVE now particularly, though as briefly as I well could, explained those words of the apostle Paul, which have been the occasion of fears and scruples in the minds of many, with respect to their attendance on the institution of the supper, and restrained them from coming to it. It only remains, as was proposed,

II. To make a few remarks, upon what has been offered, tending to remove away these fears and scruples, and make the way of those clear to the table of the Lord, who have been kept from it, by the influence of them. And,

1. IT is obvious to collect, from the explanation we have given of the apostle's words, which have been the occasion of perplexity to too many, that their fears and distresses, taking rise therefrom, are altogether groundless.

Are any of you afraid to come to the sacramental supper, lest you should "eat and drink unworthily"? There is no reason for fear, lest you should come unworthily in the sense, in which this fault is charged upon the Corinthians. It is indeed morally impossible, that persons, in your serious, concerned state of mind, should come in that grossly indecent manner,

manner, which gave occasion to the words, which have been perplexing to you. However, 'tis commendable in you, as there are other ways, in which you may eat, and drink unworthily at the Lord's table, to be so far afraid as to use all due caution, that you may be welcome guests there. This is the only reasonable operation of fear, respecting this article of duty. It ought not to keep you from communion at the sacramental supper; but should rather put you upon your guard, and such endeavours as may be proper in order to your avoiding that, which is the ground of your fear. Should your fear restrain you from your duty, its operation would be faulty. It would not, in consistency with what is right and fit, answer the design of its excitement in you, unless it should prompt you to your duty, and to a care to see that it be well done.

Are any of you afraid, if you should come to the sacramental supper, that you should be " guilty of the body and blood of the Lord"? You cannot be thus guilty, unless you *sinfully* eat of that bread, and drink of that cup, which are divinely instituted signs of " the body and blood of Christ." For this is the only meaning that can, with propriety, or truth, be applied to these words. And you do well to be afraid of *sin*, whether it relates to the ordinance

dinance of the supper, or any other service of piety. Only, you should remember, and impress your minds with a serious sense of its being true, that this very fear of your's will become *sinful*, if, instead of stirring you up to the performance of duty, and a due care to perform it in a suitable manner, it at all restrains you from it; much more, if it influences you to an habitual, and total neglect of it. You say, you fear to come to the supper of the Lord, lest you should be "guilty of his body and blood". You cannot easily be thus guilty, in the sense, in which the Corinthians were. There is no danger of your using the sacramental bread and wine, which represent figuratively, " the body and blood of Christ", in the rude, factious, prophane manner they did. Any, at this day, would be ashamed of such conduct: Nor need you be afraid of being chargeable with the guilt of it. You may, it is true, be faulty in the use of the " bread and wine", which are instituted signs of the " body and blood of Christ ; and you may reasonably fear, lest you should be thus faulty. But what ought to be the effect of this fear? Most certainly, not disobedience to as plain, and peremptory, a command as any in the bible ; but caution, watchfulness, and circumspection, that you may comply with it, in the best manner you can.

ARE any of you afraid of being chargeable with the guilt of "not difcerning the Lord's body" fhould you come to the ordinance of the fupper? You muft be grofsly ignorant, if you do not know, that there is a great and wide difference betwixt *facramental* and *common* bread and wine. And the way, now in ufe, of eating and drinking *facramental* bread and wine, is fo different from that in which it was done by the Corinthians, when thefe words were wrote, that it cannot be fuppofed you could be guilty of "not difcerning the Lord's body", in the fenfe that they were : For which reafon, a fear of this guilt, in the minds of any, is wholly groundlefs. Not but that there may be fear, and juftly too, left the *facramental* bread and wine fhould not, in the exercife of faith, be difcriminated from that which is *common*, ate and drank in a manner becoming their confecration to fo folemn a ufe as that of remembering the dying love of Chrift. But it would be altogther befide the proper and juft tendency of this fear, to keep any from partaking of this bread and wine. Its only influence fhould be to difpofe, and engage all to a due care to eat, and drink of them, agreably to the nature, and end, of fo facred an inftitution.

IN fine here, are any of you afraid of coming

ming to the holy supper, lest you should "eat and drink *damnation* to yourselves? Your fear, so far as it takes rise from the english word, *damnation*, has no just reason for its support. For, it is not expressive of what the apostle Paul means by the greek word *Krima*, he here uses; as has, I trust, been already made abundantly to appear.

Not but that "eating, and drinking unworthily", at the Lord's table, exposes to "damnation", meaning by it damnation to wrath in the future world; and you may reasonably fear so eating and drinking, as to render yourselves liable to this awful punishment: Not indeed because this punishment is the *special judgment* intended by the apostle; but because it is the punishment elsewhere, in scripture, threatned against sin in general, be its kind, or degree, what it may. For the same reason, therefore, that you are afraid of coming to the Lord's-Supper, lest by doing this unworthily, you should "eat and drink damnation to yourselves", you should fear lest, by an *unworthy neglect* of this ordinance, you should expose yourselves to this same punishment. For the truth is, there is as real danger of incurring damnation by a neglect of this instance of duty, as by an unworthy performance of it. You, who fear to come to the sacramental supper, lest you ex-

pose

pose yourselves to damnation, while, at the same time, you have no fear upon your minds, lest, by the neglect of this sacred institution, you should as justly make yourselves liable to the same punishment, would do well seriously to consider this. There is like danger in both cases; and you will only delude yourselves, if you think to avoid the danger of eating and drinking unworthily, by not eating and drinking at all.

It may, perhaps, be said here, the apostle Paul has particularly denounced damnation against *unworthiness* at the Lord's-Supper, while neither he, nor any of the sacred pen-men, have, with like particularity, pointed out this punishment, in case of not coming to it. The answer is obvious, and, as I imagine, intirely satisfactory. The apostle, in the words referred to, is speaking, as has been made evident, of temporal judgment, and inflicted only with a salutary view, in a way of fatherly chastisement; not of damnation, meaning by it punishment beyond the grave: Nor is this kind of punishment denounced any where, in the bible, against unworthy receiving the sacrament, but in those texts which denounce this same wrath against the *neglect of duty*, as well as the unworthy performance of it. So that a disobedient neglect of that supper which has been solemnly appointed by Jesus Christ, does as really expose to damnation, as an undue attendance at it. Why then should any abstain from sacramental eating and drinking, through fear, lest they should eat and drink unworthily? Sin lies at the door in either case, and danger too. And it is, without all doubt, both *more sinful*, and *more dangerous*, with respect to the persons whose fears I have been endeavouring to remove, to *neglect coming* to the sacramental supper, than to come to it with that imagined *unworthiness* which keeps them from it.

2. ANOTHER remark is this, that, should any have unhappily attended the ordinance of the supper in an unworthy manner, the best advice to them is, not to cease from attending their duty in this special instance; but to take proper care to perform it better for time to come. This remark naturally arises from the general tenor of the apostle's discourse, in the chapter we have been considering. He had been blaming, and rebuking, the church at Corinth for their rude, disorderly, and prophane manner of celebrating the holy supper. And what does he hereupon advise them to? Does he forbid them the use of this gospel ordinance? Does he say any thing tending to discourage them from going again to it? Not a word
of

of this nature is to be seen in any part of what he has wrote to them. Far from this, though they had come to the supper of the Lord with such indecency, and irreverence, as are not known in the present age, he supposes it to be their duty still to come to it; and what he endeavours is, to engage them, by proper arguments, to reform what had been amiss, and to attend their duty in a suitable manner in time to come. Christian professors would act wisely in taking due notice of the apostle's care, that the holy supper might not be neglected, and, at the same time, that it might not be unworthily celebrated. Should they be conscious, that they have waited upon Christ at his table in an unbecoming manner, they should not be discouraged, through fear, from waiting upon him again; but should rather be excited to give the more earnest heed, to get their unworthiness removed, that they may attend their duty conformably to the will of their Lord for the future.

I MAY not improperly add here, if any of those are seriously thoughtful of coming to the supper of the Lord, who have never as yet been there, they should not be discouraged from their duty, in this respect, by the influence of fear, lest they should come unworthily. Their fear should not drive them away from this ordinance,

ance, but rather put them upon the use of proper pains, that they may come in a worthy manner. The Corinthians had been guilty of schism, rudeness, and intemperance in their celebration of the sacramental supper; and yet, the apostle does not advise them to lay aside the use of this ordinance, but to take care to come to it, for the future, in a worthy manner. And this is the best advise that can be given christians at this day. It is not allowable for them to treat this ordinance with constructive contempt, by abstaining from the use it; and if they are afraid of coming to it unworthily, the effect of their fear should be, their more diligent endeavour to come in the manner they would desire, and as may be for the honor of their Lord.

3. ANOTHER remark still may be, that it ought not to be supposed, that the apostle Paul, in the chapter we have been explaining, had it in his heart to discourage those christians, from an attendance at the sacramental table, who discourage themselves, and from what he has said too. Let us attend a little to their character, more especially as drawn from the ground of their discouragement. Why are they kept back from remembering their Lord, in the way of his appointment? Is it not because they fear, lest they should not

do

do this with that faith, love, humility, and holy reverence, which become a sacred institution of gospel worship? Is it not because they have worthy sentiments of Jesus Christ, who has appointed the sacramental supper, and would willingly be communicants at it, but that they have scruples in their minds, as to their fitness to be so? Is it not because they are jealous over themselves with a Godly jealousy, jealous of the honour of their Lord, and would serve him with their best? Is it not because they are heartily desirous of pleasing Christ, and are afraid, left they should fail of doing so, should they come to his table?

CAN it now be imagined, with any face of reason, that it was the design of the apostle, by any thing he has said, in this chapter, to discourage this kind of persons from giving their presence at the sacramental supper? Could it have entered his heart to block up their way to the table of the Lord? It ought not to be supposed. Surely, if he did not discourage the Corinthians from attending this ordinance, though they came to it in such an irreverent manner, as that they were visited by God, FOR THIS VERY CAUSE, with "weakness, sickness and death," he could never intend to throw any discouragement in the way of the persons I have described. And if he could know how

how they have misconstrued his words, and taken occasion, from them, to neglect the supper of the Lord, he would scarce be able, though in heaven, to refrain from grief. And could he now speak to them from the excellent glory, it would be to advise them forthwith to lay aside their fears and scruples, and honor their Lord by celebrating the memorial of his death.

4. THE last remark is, that it should be the serious endeavor of all to come worthily to the table of Christ. The apostle Paul aimed mainly at this, in all that he said to the Corinthians, in that part of his epistle to them we have been considering. To this end he set before them their faults, and gave them the directions proper, in order to their rectifying them, that they might come to the supper Christ had appointed, not to condemnation, but to praise and honor. And this should be the care also of all, who profess themselves the disciples of Jesus. They should not esteem it a matter of trifling concern, how they partake of the symbols of their Lord's death, but should endeavor to do it, so as to glorify God, and promote their own spiritual advantage.

MANY, I am sensible, would be glad to come to the sacramental supper who were never there; and what has kept them back is, this
matter

matter of worthily partaking there. Being convinced, that they ought to come worthily, they are restrained from coming, because they fear they shall not be able thus to come. But this is a difficulty that will as truly hold against all the other duties of religion. They ought all to be performed in a worthy manner; and if persons should imagine they cannot thus perform them, why may they not as reasonably leave them all undone, as this of remembering their Savior at his supper? Is this right? What must be the effect of such conduct but a total disregard to all the services of piety? The exact truth is, the influence of fear, respecting the supper of the Lord should never be, to keep us from it, but to excite our care that we may be welcome guests at this gospel feast; and thus we shall be, if the subjects of that meetness, which is suited to the nature and design of the duty. And this meetness, I will venture to say, those are certainly possessed of, who are most sensible of their unworthiness, and most fearful lest they should dishonour Christ, by an undue attendance at his table. With respect to persons of this character, there is no danger of their rudely, or irreverently, rushing upon this ordinance. They are the men, who are most concerned, that they may be prepared for a due

due approach to it ; and there is no doubt but they ought to be ranked among those, who would be most welcome to it.

I have now said all that I had in view to say, in the choice of the subject I have been so long upon. I have, in as plain and faithful manner as I could, laid before you the obligations christians are under to celebrate the instituted memorial of their Lord's dying love. I have been particular in speaking to the careless and secure ; the lukewarm and indifferent ; the conscientious and careful, in regard of their attendance on the other institutions of gospel worship ; and, in fine, the scrupulous and fearful : endeavouring to consider, and remove, all the doubts, difficulties and fears, which have kept any from an attendance at the table of Christ, so far, at least, as they have come within reach of my knowledge.

What will be the effect of my having been thus large, and full, in treating upon this special article of christian duty, is known to God only. If what has been discoursed may, under the divine blessing, be influential upon any to do honor to their Savior, by remembering him in the way he has prescribed, it will be labor spent to good purpose. It will occasion joy of heart to all the friends of Jesus ; yea, it will be pleasing to him, who loved us, and died for us ; yea, it will be a pleasure to that God, who so loved us, even while we were sinners, as to give his only begotten Son to be slain a sacrifice to atone for our transgressions. But if what has been said should prove labor in vain, as being followed with no good effect, as having no influence to prevail upon any to join with their christian friends in breaking of that bread, which is the symbol of Christ's broken body, it will be remembered another day, that you have been faithfully entreated, warned, directed, and encouraged to the practice of this article of duty ; and you will be the more inexcusable on this account. I shall only say, I have delivered my soul, and have done it faithfully in this instance, however defective I may have been in others. The good God grant, that this christian point of practice, which has been seriously and solemnly urged, may prove a favor of life unto life unto many, and not of death unto death—to any one soul.

FINIS.

www.ingramcontent.com/pod-product-compliance
Lightning Source LLC
Chambersburg PA
CBHW030307170426
43202CB00009B/902